GOD'S PROMISES®
FOR
GRADUATES
2018

NIV

Compiled by Jack Countryman

COUNTRYMAN®

A Division of Thomas Nelson Publishers

THOMAS NELSON
Since 1798

God's Promises® for Graduates: Class of 2018
© 2018 by Jack Countryman

Published in Nashville, Tennessee, by Thomas Nelson. Thomas Nelson is a registered trademark of
HarperCollins Christian Publishing, Inc.

God's Promises® is a registered trademark of Thomas Nelson.

Thomas Nelson titles may be purchased in bulk for educational,
business, fund-raising, or sales promotional use. For information,
please e-mail SpecialMarkets@ThomasNelson.com.

Scripture quotations marked NIV are taken from the Holy Bible, New International Version®,
NIV®. Copyright © 1973, 1978, 1984, 2011 by Biblica, Inc.® Used by permission of Zondervan. All
rights reserved worldwide. www.zondervan.com. The "NIV" and "New International Version"
are trademarks registered in the United States Patent and Trademark Office by Biblica, Inc.®

ISBN 978-0-7180-7463-0 (black NIV)
ISBN 978-1-4041-0682-6 (black NIV CU)
ISBN 978-1-4003-0920-7 (lavender NIV)
ISBN 978-1-4041-0683-3 (lavender NIV CU)

Printed in China

18 19 20 21 22 TIMS 5 4 3 2 1

CONTENTS

Congratulations, graduate! You've finished one journey, and now you're starting a new one. This book is a guide for the adventures ahead.

Whatever challenges you encounter, God has promised to help you. When your faith is tested or circumstances are uncertain, you can rest confident in these guarantees from God's Word. Read them. Meditate on them. Let them soak into your spirit. And then, with God as your perfect companion, every adventure of your life will be better than you've ever imagined.

*The LORD your God will bless you
just as he has promised.*

DEUTERONOMY 15:6

WHAT TO DO
WHEN YOU NEED...

- To Make a Change (to Please God)
- Comfort
- Confidence
- Contentment
- To Make a Decision
- Discipline
- Encouragement
- Faith
- Forgiveness
- Friendship
- Guidance
- Healing
- Hope
- Humility
- Peace
- Protection
- Repentance
- To Wait on the Lord
- Wisdom

TO MAKE A CHANGE
(TO PLEASE GOD)

Therefore, if anyone is in Christ, the new creation has come: The old has gone, the new is here!

2 CORINTHIANS 5:17

"I will give them a heart to know me, that I am the LORD. They will be my people, and I will be their God, for they will return to me with all their heart."

JEREMIAH 24:7

Yet to all who did receive him, to those who believed in his name, he gave the right to become children of God—children born not of natural descent, nor of human decision or a husband's will, but born of God.

JOHN 1:12–13

"I am the true vine, and my Father is the gardener. He cuts off every branch in me that bears no fruit, while every branch that does bear fruit he prunes so that it will be even more fruitful. You are already clean because of the word I have spoken to you. Remain in me, as I also remain in you. No branch can bear fruit by itself; it must remain in the vine. Neither can you bear fruit unless you remain in me.

"I am the vine; you are the branches. If you remain in me and I in you, you will bear much fruit; apart from me you can do nothing."

JOHN 15:1–5

But when the kindness and love of God our Savior appeared, he saved us, not because of righteous things we had done, but because of his mercy. He saved us through the washing of rebirth and renewal by the Holy Spirit, whom he poured out on us generously through Jesus Christ our Savior.

TITUS 3:4–6

Therefore, as God's chosen people, holy and dearly loved, clothe yourselves with compassion, kindness, humility, gentleness and patience.

COLOSSIANS 3:12

Therefore, my dear friends, as you have always obeyed—not only in my presence, but now much more in my absence—continue to work out your salvation with fear and trembling, for it is God who works in you to will and to act in order to fulfill his good purpose.

PHILIPPIANS 2:12–13

Not that I have already obtained all this, or have already arrived at my goal, but I press on to take hold of that for which Christ Jesus took hold of me. Brothers and sisters, I do not consider myself yet to have taken hold of it. But one thing I do: Forgetting what is behind and straining toward what is ahead, I press on toward the goal to win the prize for which God has called me heavenward in Christ Jesus.

PHILIPPIANS 3:12–14

You heard about Christ and were taught in him in accordance with the truth that is in Jesus. You were taught, with regard to your former way of life, to put off your old self, which is being corrupted by its deceitful desires; to be made new in the attitude of your minds; and to put on the new self, created to be like God in true righteousness and holiness.

EPHESIANS 4:21–24

Follow God's example, therefore, as dearly loved children and walk in the way of love, just as Christ loved us and gave himself up for us as a fragrant offering and sacrifice to God.

EPHESIANS 5:1–2

For if you live according to the flesh, you will die; but if by the Spirit you put to death the misdeeds of the body, you will live.

For those who are led by the Spirit of God are the children of God.

ROMANS 8:13–14

Therefore, I urge you, brothers and sisters, in view of God's mercy, to offer your bodies as a living sacrifice, holy and pleasing to God—this is your true and proper worship. Do not conform to the pattern of this world, but be transformed by the renewing of your mind. Then you will be able to test and approve what God's will is— his good, pleasing and perfect will.

ROMANS 12:1–2

COMFORT

Yet I am always with you;
 you hold me by my right hand.

PSALM 73:23

Remember your word to your servant,
 for you have given me hope.
My comfort in my suffering is this:
 Your promise preserves my life. . . .
I remember, LORD, your ancient laws,
 and I find comfort in them.

PSALM 119:49–50, 52

Cast your cares on the LORD
 and he will sustain you;
he will never let
 the righteous be shaken.

PSALM 55:22

And we know that in all things God works for the good of those who love him, who have been called according to his purpose.

ROMANS 8:28

"I will ask the Father, and he will give you another advocate to help you and be with you forever."

JOHN 14:16

"Blessed are those who mourn,
  for they will be comforted."

MATTHEW 5:4

Praise be to the God and Father of our Lord Jesus Christ, the Father of compassion and the God of all comfort, who comforts us in all our troubles, so that we can comfort those in any trouble with the comfort we ourselves receive from God.

2 CORINTHIANS 1:3–4

For our light and momentary troubles are achieving for us an eternal glory that far outweighs them all. So we fix our eyes not on what is seen, but on what is unseen, since what is seen is temporary, but what is unseen is eternal.

2 CORINTHIANS 4:17–18

But he said to me, "My grace is sufficient for you, for my power is made perfect in weakness." Therefore I will boast all the more gladly about my weaknesses, so that Christ's power may rest on me. That is why, for Christ's sake, I delight in weaknesses, in insults, in hardships, in persecutions, in difficulties. For when I am weak, then I am strong.

2 CORINTHIANS 12:9–10

"Come to me, all you who are weary and burdened, and I will give you rest."

MATTHEW 11:28

CONFIDENCE

Let us then approach God's throne of grace with confidence, so that we may receive mercy and find grace to help us in our time of need.

HEBREWS 4:16

So do not throw away your confidence; it will be richly rewarded.

You need to persevere so that when you have done the will of God, you will receive what he has promised.

HEBREWS 10:35–36

So we say with confidence,
"The Lord is my helper; I will not be afraid.
What can mere mortals do to me?"

HEBREWS 13:6

For the Spirit God gave us does not make us timid, but gives us power, love and self-discipline.

2 TIMOTHY 1:7

Dear friends, if our hearts do not condemn us, we have confidence before God and receive from him anything we ask, because we keep his commands and do what pleases him.

1 JOHN 3:21–22

"But blessed is the one who trusts in the Lord,
whose confidence is in him."

JEREMIAH 17:7

Have no fear of sudden disaster
    or of the ruin that overtakes the wicked,
for the Lord will be at your side
    and will keep your foot from being snared.

PROVERBS 3:25–26

Being confident of this, that he who began a good work in you will carry it on to completion until the day of Christ Jesus.

PHILIPPIANS 1:6

Finally, be strong in the Lord and in his mighty power. Put on the full armor of God, so that you can take your stand against the devil's schemes.

EPHESIANS 6:10–11

CONTENTMENT

Keep your lives free from the love of money and be
content with what you have, because God has said,
　　"Never will I leave you;
　　　　never will I forsake you."
So we say with confidence,
　　"The Lord is my helper; I will not be afraid.
　　　　What can mere mortals do to me?"

HEBREWS 13:5–6

I am not saying this because I am in need, for I have
learned to be content whatever the circumstances. I
know what it is to be in need, and I know what it is to
have plenty. I have learned the secret of being content
in any and every situation, whether well fed or hungry,
whether living in plenty or in want. I can do all this
through him who gives me strength.

PHILIPPIANS 4:11–13

The fear of the LORD leads to life;
　　then one rests content, untouched by trouble.

PROVERBS 19:23

"Do not store up for yourselves treasures on earth, where moths and vermin destroy, and where thieves break in and steal. But store up for yourselves treasures in heaven, where moths and vermin do not destroy, and where thieves do not break in and steal. For where your treasure is, there your heart will be also."

MATTHEW 6:19–21

How much better to get wisdom than gold,
    to get insight rather than silver!

PROVERBS 16:16

"But seek first his kingdom and his righteousness, and all these things will be given to you as well."

MATTHEW 6:33

"Are not two sparrows sold for a penny? Yet not one of them will fall to the ground outside your Father's care. And even the very hairs of your head are all numbered. So don't be afraid; you are worth more than many sparrows."

MATTHEW 10:29–31

TO MAKE A DECISION

The fear of the Lord is the beginning of wisdom;
   all who follow his precepts have good
      understanding.
   To him belongs eternal praise.

PSALM 111:10

Therefore, I urge you, brothers and sisters, in view of God's mercy, to offer your bodies as a living sacrifice, holy and pleasing to God—this is your true and proper worship. Do not conform to the pattern of this world, but be transformed by the renewing of your mind. Then you will be able to test and approve what God's will is— his good, pleasing and perfect will.

ROMANS 12:1–2

Commit to the Lord whatever you do,
   and he will establish your plans.

PROVERBS 16:3

Trust in the Lord with all your heart
   and lean not on your own understanding;
in all your ways submit to him,
   and he will make your paths straight.

PROVERBS 3:5–6

I will instruct you and teach you in the way you
    should go;
    I will counsel you with my loving eye on you.

PSALM 32:8

Do not be anxious about anything, but in every
situation, by prayer and petition, with thanksgiving,
present your requests to God. And the peace of God,
which transcends all understanding, will guard your
hearts and your minds in Christ Jesus.

PHILIPPIANS 4:6–7

Blessed is the one
    who does not walk in step with the wicked
or stand in the way that sinners take
    or sit in the company of mockers,
but whose delight is in the law of the LORD,
    and who meditates on his law day and night.

PSALM 1:1–2

DISCIPLINE

Surely it was for my benefit
    that I suffered such anguish.
In your love you kept me
    from the pit of destruction;
you have put all my sins
    behind your back.

ISAIAH 38:17

   Have nothing to do with godless myths and old wives'
tales; rather, train yourself to be godly. For physical
training is of some value, but godliness has value for all
things, holding promise for both the present life and the
life to come.

1 TIMOTHY 4:7–8

   But if we hope for what we do not yet have, we wait
for it patiently.
   In the same way, the Spirit helps us in our weakness.
We do not know what we ought to pray for, but the
Spirit himself intercedes for us through wordless groans.

ROMANS 8:25–26

Do you not know that in a race all the runners run, but only one gets the prize? Run in such a way as to get the prize. . . .

Therefore I do not run like someone running aimlessly; I do not fight like a boxer beating the air. No, I strike a blow to my body and make it my slave so that after I have preached to others, I myself will not be disqualified for the prize.

1 Corinthians 9:24, 26–27

No discipline seems pleasant at the time, but painful. Later on, however, it produces a harvest of righteousness and peace for those who have been trained by it.

Hebrews 12:11

Know then in your heart that as a man disciplines his son, so the Lord your God disciplines you.

Deuteronomy 8:5

ENCOURAGEMENT

Wait for the LORD;
>   be strong and take heart
>   and wait for the LORD.

PSALM 27:14

And we all, who with unveiled faces contemplate the Lord's glory, are being transformed into his image with ever-increasing glory, which comes from the Lord, who is the Spirit.

Therefore, since through God's mercy we have this ministry, we do not lose heart.

2 CORINTHIANS 3:18–4:1

"He will wipe every tear from their eyes. There will be no more death' or mourning or crying or pain, for the old order of things has passed away."

He who was seated on the throne said, "I am making everything new!" Then he said, "Write this down, for these words are trustworthy and true."

He said to me: "It is done. I am the Alpha and the Omega, the Beginning and the End. To the thirsty I will give water without cost from the spring of the water of life. Those who are victorious will inherit all this, and I will be their God and they will be my children."

REVELATION 21:4–7

Let us not become weary in doing good, for at the proper time we will reap a harvest if we do not give up.

GALATIANS 6:9

Do not be anxious about anything, but in every situation, by prayer and petition, with thanksgiving, present your requests to God. And the peace of God, which transcends all understanding, will guard your hearts and your minds in Christ Jesus.

PHILIPPIANS 4:6–7

FAITH

"Have I not commanded you? Be strong and courageous. Do not be afraid; do not be discouraged, for the LORD your God will be with you wherever you go."

JOSHUA 1:9

In all this you greatly rejoice, though now for a little while you may have had to suffer grief in all kinds of trials. These have come so that the proven genuineness of your faith—of greater worth than gold, which perishes even though refined by fire—may result in praise, glory and honor when Jesus Christ is revealed.

1 PETER 1:6–7

For in the gospel the righteousness of God is revealed—a righteousness that is by faith from first to last, just as it is written: "The righteous will live by faith."

ROMANS 1:17

Consequently, faith comes from hearing the message, and the message is heard through the word about Christ.

ROMANS 10:17

He replied, "If you have faith as small as a mustard seed, you can say to this mulberry tree, 'Be uprooted and planted in the sea,' and it will obey you."

LUKE 17:6

So then, just as you received Christ Jesus as Lord, continue to live your lives in him, rooted and built up in him, strengthened in the faith as you were taught, and overflowing with thankfulness.

COLOSSIANS 2:6–7

For it is by grace you have been saved, through faith—and this is not from yourselves, it is the gift of God—not by works, so that no one can boast.

EPHESIANS 2:8–9

Consider it pure joy, my brothers and sisters, whenever you face trials of many kinds, because you know that the testing of your faith produces perseverance.

JAMES 1:2–3

Fight the good fight of the faith. Take hold of the eternal life to which you were called when you made your good confession in the presence of many witnesses.

1 TIMOTHY 6:12

"So do not fear, for I am with you;
    do not be dismayed, for I am your God.
I will strengthen you and help you;
    I will uphold you with my righteous right hand."

ISAIAH 41:10

FORGIVENESS

If we confess our sins, he is faithful and just and will forgive us our sins and purify us from all unrighteousness.

1 JOHN 1:9

My dear children, I write this to you so that you will not sin. But if anybody does sin, we have an advocate with the Father—Jesus Christ, the Righteous One. He is the atoning sacrifice for our sins, and not only for ours but also for the sins of the whole world.

1 JOHN 2:1–2

Therefore, as God's chosen people, holy and dearly loved, clothe yourselves with compassion, kindness, humility, gentleness and patience. Bear with each other and forgive one another if any of you has a grievance against someone. Forgive as the Lord forgave you.

COLOSSIANS 3:12–13

Seek the LORD while he may be found;
    call on him while he is near.
Let the wicked forsake their ways
    and the unrighteous their thoughts.
Let them turn to the LORD, and he will have mercy
    on them,
    and to our God, for he will freely pardon.

ISAIAH 55:6–7

In him we have redemption through his blood, the forgiveness of sins, in accordance with the riches of God's grace that he lavished on us. With all wisdom and understanding.

Ephesians 1:7–8

"Come now, let us settle the matter,"
    says the Lord.
"Though your sins are like scarlet,
    they shall be as white as snow;
though they are red as crimson,
    they shall be like wool."

Isaiah 1:18

Therefore, there is now no condemnation for those who are in Christ Jesus, because through Christ Jesus the law of the Spirit who gives life has set you free from the law of sin and death.

Romans 8:1–2

FRIENDSHIP

One who has unreliable friends soon comes to ruin,
  but there is a friend who sticks closer than a
  brother.

PROVERBS 18:24

A friend loves at all times,
  and a brother is born for a time of adversity.

PROVERBS 17:17

May the God who gives endurance and
encouragement give you the same attitude of mind
toward each other that Christ Jesus had, so that with one
mind and one voice you may glorify the God and Father
of our Lord Jesus Christ.

Accept one another, then, just as Christ accepted you,
in order to bring praise to God.

ROMANS 15:5–7

And my God will meet all your needs according to the
riches of his glory in Christ Jesus.

PHILIPPIANS 4:19

Perfume and incense bring joy to the heart,
  and the pleasantness of a friend
  springs from their heartfelt advice.

PROVERBS 27:9

"You are my friends if you do what I command. I no longer call you servants, because a servant does not know his master's business. Instead, I have called you friends, for everything that I learned from my Father I have made known to you."

JOHN 15:14–15

GUIDANCE

If any of you lacks wisdom, you should ask God, who gives generously to all without finding fault, and it will be given to you. But when you ask, you must believe and not doubt, because the one who doubts is like a wave of the sea, blown and tossed by the wind.

JAMES 1:5–6

I lift up my eyes to the mountains—
    where does my help come from?
My help comes from the LORD,
    the Maker of heaven and earth.

PSALM 121:1–2

The LORD himself goes before you and will be with you; he will never leave you nor forsake you. Do not be afraid; do not be discouraged.

DEUTERONOMY 31:8

He guides the humble in what is right
    and teaches them his way.

PSALM 25:9

"But when he, the Spirit of truth, comes, he will guide you into all the truth. He will not speak on his own; he will speak only what he hears, and he will tell you what is yet to come."

JOHN 16:13

The LORD makes firm the steps
of the one who delights in him.

PSALM 37:23

LORD, I know that people's lives are not their own;
it is not for them to direct their steps.

JEREMIAH 10:23

Whether you turn to the right or to the left, your
ears will hear a voice behind you, saying, "This is the
way; walk in it."

ISAIAH 30:21

May the Lord direct your hearts into God's love and
Christ's perseverance.

2 THESSALONIANS 3:5

HEALING

Is anyone among you in trouble? Let them pray. Is anyone happy? Let them sing songs of praise. Is anyone among you sick? Let them call the elders of the church to pray over them and anoint them with oil in the name of the Lord. And the prayer offered in faith will make the sick person well; the Lord will raise them up. If they have sinned, they will be forgiven. Therefore confess your sins to each other and pray for each other so that you may be healed. The prayer of a righteous person is powerful and effective.

JAMES 5:13–16

"Worship the LORD your God, and his blessing will be on your food and water. I will take away sickness from among you, and none will miscarry or be barren in your land. I will give you a full life span."

EXODUS 23:25–26

"But for you who revere my name, the sun of righteousness will rise with healing in its rays. And you will go out and frolic like well-fed calves."

MALACHI 4:2

Praise the LORD, my soul,
  and forget not all his benefits—
who forgives all your sins
  and heals all your diseases.

PSALM 103:2–3

LORD my God, I called to you for help,
  and you healed me.

PSALM 30:2

The righteous person may have many troubles,
  but the LORD delivers him from them all.

PSALM 34:19

"He himself bore our sins" in his body on the cross, so
that we might die to sins and live for righteousness; "by
his wounds you have been healed."

1 PETER 2:24

HOPE

And God is able to bless you abundantly, so that in all things at all times, having all that you need, you will abound in every good work.

2 CORINTHIANS 9:8

Why, my soul, are you downcast?
    Why so disturbed within me?
Put your hope in God,
    for I will yet praise him,
    my Savior and my God.

PSALM 42:5

"For I know the plans I have for you," declares the LORD, "plans to prosper you and not to harm you, plans to give you hope and a future."

JEREMIAH 29:11

Praise be to the God and Father of our Lord Jesus Christ! In his great mercy he has given us new birth into a living hope through the resurrection of Jesus Christ from the dead.

1 PETER 1:3

Do you not know?
　　Have you not heard?
The LORD is the everlasting God,
　　the Creator of the ends of the earth.
He will not grow tired or weary,
　　and his understanding no one can fathom.
He gives strength to the weary
　　and increases the power of the weak.
Even youths grow tired and weary,
　　and young men stumble and fall;
but those who hope in the LORD
　　will renew their strength.
They will soar on wings like eagles;
　　they will run and not grow weary,
　　they will walk and not be faint.

ISAIAH 40:28–31

Blessed are those whose help is the God of Jacob,
　　whose hope is in the LORD their God.
He is the Maker of heaven and earth,
　　the sea, and everything in them—
　　he remains faithful forever.

PSALM 146:5–6

The LORD delights in those who fear him,
　　who put their hope in his unfailing love.

PSALM 147:11

HUMILITY

Wisdom's instruction is to fear the LORD,
  and humility comes before honor.

PROVERBS 15:33

Humility is the fear of the LORD;
  its wages are riches and honor and life.

PROVERBS 22:4

Let someone else praise you, and not your own mouth;
  an outsider, and not your own lips.

PROVERBS 27:2

"Has not my hand made all these things,
  and so they came into being?"
    declares the LORD.
"These are the ones I look on with favor:
  those who are humble and contrite in spirit,
  and who tremble at my word."

ISAIAH 66:2

For by the grace given me I say to every one of you: Do not think of yourself more highly than you ought, but rather think of yourself with sober judgment, in accordance with the faith God has distributed to each of you.

ROMANS 12:3

"For all those who exalt themselves will be humbled, and those who humble themselves will be exalted."

LUKE 14:11

Humble yourselves, therefore, under God's mighty hand, that he may lift you up in due time. Cast all your anxiety on him because he cares for you.

1 PETER 5:6–7

PEACE

Let the peace of Christ rule in your hearts, since as members of one body you were called to peace. And be thankful.

Colossians 3:15

The Lord is near. Do not be anxious about anything, but in every situation, by prayer and petition, with thanksgiving, present your requests to God. And the peace of God, which transcends all understanding, will guard your hearts and your minds in Christ Jesus.

Philippians 4:5–7

In peace I will lie down and sleep,
   for you alone, Lord,
   make me dwell in safety.

Psalm 4:8

"I have told you these things, so that in me you may have peace. In this world you will have trouble. But take heart! I have overcome the world."

John 16:33

You will keep in perfect peace
    those whose minds are steadfast,
    because they trust in you.
Trust in the Lord forever,
    for the Lord, the Lord himself, is the Rock
    eternal.

ISAIAH 26:3–4

I will listen to what God the Lord says;
    he promises peace to his people, his faithful
    servants—
    but let them not turn to folly.

PSALM 85:8

When the Lord takes pleasure in anyone's way,
    he causes their enemies to make peace with them.

PROVERBS 16:7

"Peace I leave with you; my peace I give you. I do not
give to you as the world gives. Do not let your hearts be
troubled and do not be afraid."

JOHN 14:27

Turn from evil and do good;
    seek peace and pursue it.
The eyes of the Lord are on the righteous,
    and his ears are attentive to their cry.

PSALM 34:14–15

"The Lord bless you
    and keep you;
the Lord make his face shine on you
    and be gracious to you;
the Lord turn his face toward you
    and give you peace."

NUMBERS 6:24–26

PROTECTION

My shield is God Most High,
  who saves the upright in heart.

The angel of the LORD encamps around those who
  fear him,
    and he delivers them.
Taste and see that the LORD is good;
  blessed is the one who takes refuge in him.

PSALM 34:7–8

If you say, "The LORD is my refuge,"
  and you make the Most High your dwelling,
no harm will overtake you,
  no disaster will come near your tent.
For he will command his angels concerning you
  to guard you in all your ways.

PSALM 91:9–11

When you lie down, you will not be afraid;
  when you lie down, your sleep will be sweet.
Have no fear of sudden disaster
  or of the ruin that overtakes the wicked,
for the LORD will be at your side
  and will keep your foot from being snared.

PROVERBS 3:24–26

"When you pass through the waters,
   I will be with you;
and when you pass through the rivers,
   they will not sweep over you.
When you walk through the fire,
   you will not be burned;
   the flames will not set you ablaze."

ISAIAH 43:2

"I will make you a wall to this people,
   a fortified wall of bronze;
they will fight against you
   but will not overcome you,
for I am with you
   to rescue and save you,"
      declares the LORD.
"I will save you from the hands of the wicked
   and deliver you from the grasp of the cruel."

JEREMIAH 15:20–21

"Have I not commanded you? Be strong and courageous. Do not be afraid; do not be discouraged, for the LORD your God will be with you wherever you go."

JOSHUA 1:9

REPENTANCE

"If my people, who are called by my name, will humble themselves and pray and seek my face and turn from their wicked ways, then I will hear from heaven, and I will forgive their sin and will heal their land."

2 CHRONICLES 7:14

Jesus answered them, "It is not the healthy who need a doctor, but the sick. I have not come to call the righteous, but sinners to repentance."

LUKE 5:31–32

Seek the LORD while he may be found;
    call on him while he is near.
Let the wicked forsake their ways
    and the unrighteous their thoughts.
Let them turn to the LORD, and he will have mercy
  on them,
    and to our God, for he will freely pardon.

ISAIAH 55:6–7

Then I acknowledged my sin to you
    and did not cover up my iniquity.
I said, "I will confess
    my transgressions to the LORD."
And you forgave
    the guilt of my sin.

PSALM 32:5

Whoever conceals their sins does not prosper,
    but the one who confesses and renounces them
      finds mercy.

PROVERBS 28:13

Godly sorrow brings repentance that leads to salvation and leaves no regret, but worldly sorrow brings death.

2 CORINTHIANS 7:10

But do not forget this one thing, dear friends: With the Lord a day is like a thousand years, and a thousand years are like a day. The Lord is not slow in keeping his promise, as some understand slowness. Instead he is patient with you, not wanting anyone to perish, but everyone to come to repentance.

2 PETER 3:8–9

TO WAIT ON THE LORD

Humble yourselves, therefore, under God's mighty hand, that he may lift you up in due time. Cast all your anxiety on him because he cares for you.

1 PETER 5:6–7

Therefore, since we have a great high priest who has ascended into heaven, Jesus the Son of God, let us hold firmly to the faith we profess. For we do not have a high priest who is unable to empathize with our weaknesses, but we have one who has been tempted in every way, just as we are—yet he did not sin. Let us then approach God's throne of grace with confidence, so that we may receive mercy and find grace to help us in our time of need.

HEBREWS 4:14–16

The eyes of the LORD are on the righteous,
    and his ears are attentive to their cry.

PSALM 34:15

But the eyes of the LORD are on those who fear him,
    on those whose hope is in his unfailing love. . . .
We wait in hope for the LORD;
    he is our help and our shield.
In him our hearts rejoice,
    for we trust in his holy name.

PSALM 33:18, 20–21

"And call on me in the day of trouble;
    I will deliver you, and you will honor me."

PSALM 50:15

"Come to me, all you who are weary and burdened, and I will give you rest. Take my yoke upon you and learn from me, for I am gentle and humble in heart, and you will find rest for your souls. For my yoke is easy and my burden is light."

MATTHEW 11:28–30

He says, "Be still, and know that I am God;
    I will be exalted among the nations,
    I will be exalted in the earth."

PSALM 46:10

WISDOM

If any of you lacks wisdom, you should ask God, who gives generously to all without finding fault, and it will be given to you.

JAMES 1:5

The fear of the LORD is the beginning of wisdom;
    all who follow his precepts have good
        understanding.
    To him belongs eternal praise.

PSALM 111:10

What we have received is not the spirit of the world, but the Spirit who is from God, so that we may understand what God has freely given us. This is what we speak, not in words taught us by human wisdom but in words taught by the Spirit, explaining spiritual realities with Spirit-taught words.

1 CORINTHIANS 2:12–13

How much better to get wisdom than gold,
    to get insight rather than silver!

PROVERBS 16:16

Blessed are those who find wisdom,
    those who gain understanding,
for she is more profitable than silver
    and yields better returns than gold.

PROVERBS 3:13–14

He changes times and seasons;
    he deposes kings and raises up others.
He gives wisdom to the wise
    and knowledge to the discerning.

DANIEL 2:21

For the LORD gives wisdom;
    from his mouth come knowledge and
    understanding.

PROVERBS 2:6

"For I will give you words and wisdom that none of
your adversaries will be able to resist or contradict."

LUKE 21:15

WHAT TO DO
WHEN YOU FEEL...

- Angry
- Anxiety and Worry
- Depressed
- Discouraged
- Doubt
- Fear
- Guilty
- Lonely

ANGRY

My dear brothers and sisters, take note of this: Everyone should be quick to listen, slow to speak and slow to become angry, because human anger does not produce the righteousness that God desires.

JAMES 1:19–20

A gentle answer turns away wrath,
    but a harsh word stirs up anger.

PROVERBS 15:1

But now you must also rid yourselves of all such things as these: anger, rage, malice, slander, and filthy language from your lips.

COLOSSIANS 3:8

Fools give full vent to their rage,
    but the wise bring calm in the end.

PROVERBS 29:11

"In your anger do not sin": Do not let the sun go down while you are still angry, and do not give the devil a foothold.

EPHESIANS 4:26–27

Get rid of all bitterness, rage and anger, brawling and slander, along with every form of malice. Be kind and compassionate to one another, forgiving each other, just as in Christ God forgave you.

EPHESIANS 4:31–32

Tremble and do not sin;
    when you are on your beds,
    search your hearts and be silent.
Offer the sacrifices of the righteous
    and trust in the LORD.

PSALM 4:4–5

The one who has knowledge uses words with restraint,
    and whoever has understanding is even-tempered.

PROVERBS 17:27

ANXIETY AND WORRY

"Therefore I tell you, do not worry about your life, what you will eat or drink; or about your body, what you will wear. Is not life more than food, and the body more than clothes? Look at the birds of the air; they do not sow or reap or store away in barns, and yet your heavenly Father feeds them. Are you not much more valuable than they?"

MATTHEW 6:25–26

Do not be anxious about anything, but in every situation, by prayer and petition, with thanksgiving, present your requests to God. And the peace of God, which transcends all understanding, will guard your hearts and your minds in Christ Jesus.

PHILIPPIANS 4:6–7

I sought the LORD, and he answered me;
    he delivered me from all my fears.

PSALM 34:4

Humble yourselves, therefore, under God's mighty hand, that he may lift you up in due time. Cast all your anxiety on him because he cares for you.

1 PETER 5:6–7

Trust in him at all times, you people;
  pour out your hearts to him,
  for God is our refuge.

PSALM 62:8

And we know that in all things God works for the good of those who love him, who have been called according to his purpose.

ROMANS 8:28

The LORD is my light and my salvation—
  whom shall I fear?
The LORD is the stronghold of my life—
  of whom shall I be afraid?

PSALM 27:1

God is our refuge and strength,
  an ever-present help in trouble.

PSALM 46:1

"But blessed is the one who trusts in the LORD,
  whose confidence is in him.
They will be like a tree planted by the water
  that sends out its roots by the stream.
It does not fear when heat comes;
  its leaves are always green.
It has no worries in a year of drought
  and never fails to bear fruit."

JEREMIAH 17:7–8

DEPRESSED

I [Jeremiah] well remember them,
   and my soul is downcast within me.
Yet this I call to mind
   and therefore I have hope:
Because of the LORD's great love we are not
   consumed,
   for his compassions never fail.
They are new every morning;
   great is your faithfulness.

LAMENTATIONS 3:20–23

As for me, I call to God,
   and the LORD saves me.
Evening, morning and noon
   I cry out in distress,
   and he hears my voice.
He rescues me unharmed
   from the battle waged against me,
   even though many oppose me.

PSALM 55:16–18

I will praise the LORD, who counsels me;
   even at night my heart instructs me.
I keep my eyes always on the LORD.
   With him at my right hand, I will not be shaken.

PSALM 16:7–8

Trust in the LORD and do good;
    dwell in the land and enjoy safe pasture.
Take delight in the LORD,
    and he will give you the desires of your heart.
Commit your way to the LORD;
    trust in him and he will do this:
He will make your righteous reward shine like the dawn,
    your vindication like the noonday sun.

PSALM 37:3–6

Why, my soul, are you downcast?
    Why so disturbed within me?
Put your hope in God,
    for I will yet praise him,
    my Savior and my God.

PSALM 42:11

My flesh and my heart may fail,
    but God is the strength of my heart
    and my portion forever.

PSALM 73:26

Trust in the LORD with all your heart
    and lean not on your own understanding;
in all your ways submit to him,
    and he will make your paths straight.

PROVERBS 3:5–6

DISCOURAGED

Cast your cares on the LORD
 and he will sustain you;
he will never let
 the righteous be shaken.

PSALM 55:22

When I called, you answered me;
 you greatly emboldened me.

PSALM 138:3

"Have I not commanded you? Be strong and courageous. Do not be afraid; do not be discouraged, for the LORD your God will be with you wherever you go."

JOSHUA 1:9

The LORD himself goes before you and will be with you; he will never leave you nor forsake you. Do not be afraid; do not be discouraged.

DEUTERONOMY 31:8

Fight the good fight of the faith. Take hold of the eternal life to which you were called when you made your good confession in the presence of many witnesses.

1 TIMOTHY 6:12

Let us hold unswervingly to the hope we profess, for he who promised is faithful.

HEBREWS 10:23

The Lord is my strength and my shield;
    my heart trusts in him, and he helps me.
My heart leaps for joy,
    and with my song I praise him.

PSALM 28:7

Brothers and sisters, I do not consider myself yet to have taken hold of it. But one thing I do: Forgetting what is behind and straining toward what is ahead, I press on toward the goal to win the prize for which God has called me heavenward in Christ Jesus.

PHILIPPIANS 3:13–14

Then you will have success if you are careful to observe the decrees and laws that the Lord gave Moses for Israel. Be strong and courageous. Do not be afraid or discouraged.

1 CHRONICLES 22:13

DOUBT

He replied, "You of little faith, why are you so afraid?"
Then he got up and rebuked the winds and the waves,
and it was completely calm.

MATTHEW 8:26

"Do not let your hearts be troubled. You believe in
God; believe also in me."

JOHN 14:1

Now to him who is able to establish you in accordance
with my gospel, the message I proclaim about Jesus
Christ, in keeping with the revelation of the mystery
hidden for long ages past, but now revealed and made
known through the prophetic writings by the command
of the eternal God, so that all the Gentiles might come
to the obedience that comes from faith—to the only
wise God be glory forever through Jesus Christ! Amen.

ROMANS 16:25–27

But Zion said, "The Lord has forsaken me,
the Lord has forgotten me."
"Can a mother forget the baby at her breast
and have no compassion on the child she has
borne?
Though she may forget,
I will not forget you! . . .
Lift up your eyes and look around;
all your children gather and come to you.
As surely as I live," declares the Lord,
"you will wear them all as ornaments;
you will put them on, like a bride."

ISAIAH 49:14–15, 18

Your word, Lord, is eternal;
it stands firm in the heavens.

PSALM 119:89

Blessed is the one
who does not walk in step with the wicked
or stand in the way that sinners take
or sit in the company of mockers,
but whose delight is in the law of the Lord,
and who meditates on his law day and night.
That person is like a tree planted by streams of water,
which yields its fruit in season
and whose leaf does not wither—
whatever they do prospers.

PSALM 1:1–3

The grass withers and the flowers fall,
but the word of our God endures forever.

ISAIAH 40:8

But you, dear friends, by building yourselves up in
your most holy faith and praying in the Holy Spirit,
keep yourselves in God's love as you wait for the mercy
of our Lord Jesus Christ to bring you to eternal life.

JUDE VV. 20–21

For everything that was written in the past was
written to teach us, so that through the endurance
taught in the Scriptures and the encouragement they
provide we might have hope.

ROMANS 15:4

For the word of God is alive and active. Sharper
than any double-edged sword, it penetrates even to
dividing soul and spirit, joints and marrow; it judges the
thoughts and attitudes of the heart.

HEBREWS 4:12

FEAR

"So do not fear, for I am with you;
  do not be dismayed, for I am your God.
I will strengthen you and help you;
  I will uphold you with my righteous right hand."

ISAIAH 41:10

But now, this is what the LORD says—
  he who created you, Jacob,
  he who formed you, Israel:
"Do not fear, for I have redeemed you;
  I have summoned you by name; you are mine.
When you pass through the waters,
  I will be with you;
and when you pass through the rivers,
  they will not sweep over you.
When you walk through the fire,
  you will not be burned;
  the flames will not set you ablaze."

ISAIAH 43:1–2

The Spirit you received does not make you slaves, so that you live in fear again; rather, the Spirit you received brought about your adoption to sonship. And by him we cry, *"Abba*, Father." The Spirit himself testifies with our spirit that we are God's children.

ROMANS 8:15–16

I sought the LORD, and he answered me;
he delivered me from all my fears.

PSALM 34:4

The LORD is my light and my salvation—
whom shall I fear?
The LORD is the stronghold of my life—
of whom shall I be afraid?

PSALM 27:1

For the Spirit God gave us does not not make us
timid, but gives us power, love and self-discipline.

2 TIMOTHY 1:7

Even though I walk
through the darkest valley,
I will fear no evil,
for you are with me;
your rod and your staff,
they comfort me.

PSALM 23:4

When I am afraid, I put my trust in you.
In God, whose word I praise—
in God I trust and am not afraid.
What can mere mortals do to me?

PSALM 56:3–4

But whoever listens to me will live in safety
and be at ease, without fear of harm.

PROVERBS 1:33

There is no fear in love. But perfect love drives out
fear, because fear has to do with punishment. The one
who fears is not made perfect in love.

1 JOHN 4:18

GUILTY

Therefore confess your sins to each other and pray for each other so that you may be healed. The prayer of a righteous person is powerful and effective.

JAMES 5:16

Therefore, there is now no condemnation for those who are in Christ Jesus, because through Christ Jesus the law of the Spirit who gives life has set you free from the law of sin and death.

ROMANS 8:1–2

If we confess our sins, he is faithful and just and will forgive us our sins and purify us from all unrighteousness.

1 JOHN 1:9

"So if the Son sets you free, you will be free indeed."

JOHN 8:36

"I, even I, am he who blots out
    your transgressions, for my own sake,
    and remembers your sins no more."

ISAIAH 43:25

Come near to God and he will come near to you.
Wash your hands, you sinners, and purify your hearts,
you double-minded. . . . Humble yourselves before the
Lord, and he will lift you up.

JAMES 4:8, 10

Then I acknowledged my sin to you
    and did not cover up my iniquity.
I said, "I will confess
    my transgressions to the LORD."
And you forgave
    the guilt of my sin.

PSALM 32:5

"But very truly I tell you, it is for your good that I am
going away. Unless I go away, the Advocate will not
come to you; but if I go, I will send him to you. When he
comes, he will prove the world to be in the wrong about
sin and righteousness and judgment."

JOHN 16:7–8

The one who sins is the one who will die. The child
will not share the guilt of the parent, nor will the parent
share the guilt of the child. The righteousness of the
righteous will be credited to them, and the wickedness
of the wicked will be charged against them.

EZEKIEL 18:20

LONELY

Keep your lives free from the love of money and be
content with what you have, because God has said,
  "Never will I leave you;
    never will I forsake you."

HEBREWS 13:5

I waited patiently for the LORD;
  he turned to me and heard my cry.
He lifted me out of the slimy pit,
  out of the mud and mire;
he set my feet on a rock
  and gave me a firm place to stand.
He put a new song in my mouth,
  a hymn of praise to our God.
Many will see and fear the LORD
  and put their trust in him.

PSALM 40:1–3

"Surely I am with you always, to the very end of the age."

MATTHEW 28:20

A father to the fatherless, a defender of widows,
  is God in his holy dwelling.
God sets the lonely in families,
  he leads out the prisoners with singing;
    but the rebellious live in a sun-scorched land.

PSALM 68:5–6

"So do not fear, for I am with you;
do not be dismayed, for I am your God.
I will strengthen you and help you;
I will uphold you with my righteous right hand."

ISAIAH 41:10

Where can I go from your Spirit?
Where can I flee from your presence?
If I go up to the heavens, you are there;
if I make my bed in the depths, you are there.
If I rise on the wings of the dawn,
if I settle on the far side of the sea,
even there your hand will guide me,
your right hand will hold me fast.
If I say, "Surely the darkness will hide me
and the light become night around me,"
even the darkness will not be dark to you;
the night will shine like the day,
for darkness is as light to you.

PSALM 139:7–12

"Come to me, all you who are weary and burdened, and I will give you rest. Take my yoke upon you and learn from me, for I am gentle and humble in heart, and you will find rest for your souls. For my yoke is easy and my burden is light."

MATTHEW 11:28–30

WHAT THE BIBLE
HAS TO SAY ABOUT...

- Addiction
- Alienation from God
- Your Conscience
- Foul Language
- Hate
- Holiness
- The Holy Spirit
- Leading Someone to Christ
- Love of God
- Love of Others
- Marriage
- Money
- Obedience
- Overcoming Evil

ADDICTION

Therefore, brothers and sisters, we have an obligation— but it is not to the flesh, to live according to it. For if you live according to the flesh, you will die; but if by the Spirit you put to death the misdeeds of the body, you will live.

For those who are led by the Spirit of God are the children of God. The Spirit you received does not make you slaves, so that you live in fear again; rather, the Spirit you received brought about your adoption to sonship. And by him we cry, *"Abba,* Father."

ROMANS 8:12–15

No, in all these things we are more than conquerors through him who loved us.

ROMANS 8:37

Now to him who is able to do immeasurably more than all we ask or imagine, according to his power that is at work within us, to him be glory in the church and in Christ Jesus throughout all generations, for ever and ever! Amen.

EPHESIANS 3:20–21

Do you not know that your bodies are temples of the Holy Spirit, who is in you, whom you have received from God? You are not your own; you were bought at a price. Therefore honor God with your bodies.

1 CORINTHIANS 6:19–20

For we do not have a high priest who is unable to empathize with our weaknesses, but we have one who has been tempted in every way, just as we are—yet he did not sin. Let us then approach God's throne of grace with confidence, so that we may receive mercy and find grace to help us in our time of need.

HEBREWS 4:15–16

If we claim to be without sin, we deceive ourselves and the truth is not in us. If we confess our sins, he is faithful and just and will forgive us our sins and purify us from all unrighteousness.

1 JOHN 1:8–9

Jesus replied, "Very truly I tell you, everyone who sins is a slave to sin. Now a slave has no permanent place in the family, but a son belongs to it forever. So if the Son sets you free, you will be free indeed."

JOHN 8:34–36

Therefore, since we have these promises, dear friends, let us purify ourselves from everything that contaminates body and spirit, perfecting holiness out of reverence for God.

2 CORINTHIANS 7:1

But rejoice inasmuch as you participate in the sufferings of Christ, so that you may be overjoyed when his glory is revealed.

1 PETER 4:13

For this reason, since the day we heard about you, we have not stopped praying for you. We continually ask God to fill you with the knowledge of his will through all the wisdom and understanding that the Spirit gives, so that you may live a life worthy of the Lord and please him in every way: bearing fruit in every good work, growing in the knowledge of God, being strengthened with all power according to his glorious might so that you may have great endurance and patience.

COLOSSIANS 1:9–11

ALIENATION FROM GOD

For I am convinced that neither death nor life, neither angels nor demons, neither the present nor the future, nor any powers, neither height nor depth, nor anything else in all creation, will be able to separate us from the love of God that is in Christ Jesus our Lord.

ROMANS 8:38–39

Once you were alienated from God and were enemies in your minds because of your evil behavior. But now he has reconciled you by Christ's physical body through death to present you holy in his sight, without blemish and free from accusation.

COLOSSIANS 1:21–22

Hear my prayer, LORD;
    listen to my cry for mercy.
When I am in distress, I call to you,
    because you answer me.

PSALM 86:6–7

"For I know the plans I have for you," declares the LORD, "plans to prosper you and not to harm you, plans to give you hope and a future. Then you will call on me and come and pray to me, and I will listen to you. You will seek me and find me when you seek me with all your heart."

JEREMIAH 29:11–13

For this reason I kneel before the Father, from whom every family in heaven and on earth derives its name. I pray that out of his glorious riches he may strengthen you with power through his Spirit in your inner being, so that Christ may dwell in your hearts through faith. And I pray that you, being rooted and established in love, may have power, together with all the Lord's holy people, to grasp how wide and long and high and deep is the love of Christ, and to know this love that surpasses knowledge—that you may be filled to the measure of all the fullness of God.

EPHESIANS 3:14–19

But you are a chosen people, a royal priesthood, a holy nation, God's special possession, that you may declare the praises of him who called you out of darkness into his wonderful light. Once you were not a people, but now you are the people of God; once you had not received mercy, but now you have received mercy.

1 PETER 2:9–10

YOUR CONSCIENCE

But in your hearts revere Christ as Lord. Always be prepared to give an answer to everyone who asks you to give the reason for the hope that you have. But do this with gentleness and respect, keeping a clear conscience, so that those who speak maliciously against your good behavior in Christ may be ashamed of their slander.

1 PETER 3:15–16

My son, do not let wisdom and understanding out of
  your sight,
    preserve sound judgment and discretion;
they will be life for you,
    an ornament to grace your neck.
Then you will go on your way in safety,
    and your foot will not stumble.
When you lie down, you will not be afraid;
    when you lie down, your sleep will be sweet.

PROVERBS 3:21–24

How much more, then, will the blood of Christ, who through the eternal Spirit offered himself unblemished to God, cleanse our consciences from acts that lead to death, so that we may serve the living God!

HEBREWS 9:14

So I strive always to keep my conscience clear before God and man.

Let us draw near to God with a sincere heart and with the full assurance that faith brings, having our hearts sprinkled to cleanse us from a guilty conscience and having our bodies washed with pure water.

HEBREWS 10:22

Timothy, my son, I am giving you this command in keeping with the prophecies once made about you, so that by recalling them you may fight the battle well, holding on to faith and a good conscience, which some have rejected and so have suffered shipwreck with regard to the faith.

1 TIMOTHY 1:18–19

Therefore, there is now no condemnation for those who are in Christ Jesus, because through Christ Jesus the law of the Spirit who gives life has set you free from the law of sin and death.

ROMANS 8:1–2

FOUL LANGUAGE

But among you there must not be even a hint of sexual immorality, or of any kind of impurity, or of greed, because these are improper for God's holy people. Nor should there be obscenity, foolish talk or coarse joking, which are out of place, but rather thanksgiving.

EPHESIANS 5:3–4

But now you must also rid yourselves of all such things as these: anger, rage, malice, slander, and filthy language from your lips.

COLOSSIANS 3:8

Words from the mouth of the wise are gracious,
but fools are consumed by their own lips.

ECCLESIASTES 10:12

The words of the reckless pierce like swords,
but the tongue of the wise brings healing.

PROVERBS 12:18

Those who guard their mouths and their tongues
keep themselves from calamity.

PROVERBS 21:23

Let your conversation be always full of grace, seasoned with salt, so that you may know how to answer everyone.

COLOSSIANS 4:6

Do not let any unwholesome talk come out of your mouths, but only what is helpful for building others up according to their needs, that it may benefit those who listen.

EPHESIANS 4:29

Set a guard over my mouth, LORD;
    keep watch over the door of my lips.

PSALM 141:3

Those who consider themselves religious and yet do not keep a tight rein on their tongues deceive themselves, and their religion is worthless.

JAMES 1:26

"All you need to say is simply 'Yes' or 'No'; anything beyond this comes from the evil one."

MATTHEW 5:37

HATE

Get rid of all bitterness, rage and anger, brawling and slander, along with every form of malice.

EPHESIANS 4:31

You, my brothers and sisters, were called to be free. But do not use your freedom to indulge the flesh; rather, serve one another humbly in love. For the entire law is fulfilled in keeping this one command: "Love your neighbor as yourself."

GALATIANS 5:13–14

Make every effort to live in peace with everyone and to be holy; without holiness no one will see the Lord. See to it that no one falls short of the grace of God and that no bitter root grows up to cause trouble and defile many.

HEBREWS 12:14–15

Do not be overcome by evil, but overcome evil with good.

ROMANS 12:21

Because judgment without mercy will be shown to anyone who has not been merciful. Mercy triumphs over judgment.

JAMES 2:13

And so we know and rely on the love God has for us. God is love. Whoever lives in love lives in God, and God in them.

1 John 4:16

"A new command I give you: Love one another. As I have loved you, so you must love one another. By this everyone will know that you are my disciples, if you love one another."

John 13:34–35

"But to you who are listening I say: Love your enemies, do good to those who hate you, bless those who curse you, pray for those who mistreat you."

Luke 6:27–28

Love must be sincere. Hate what is evil; cling to what is good.

Romans 12:9

HOLINESS

Follow God's example, therefore, as dearly loved children and walk in the way of love, just as Christ loved us and gave himself up for us as a fragrant offering and sacrifice to God.

EPHESIANS 5:1–2

Therefore, I urge you, brothers and sisters, in view of God's mercy, to offer your bodies as a living sacrifice, holy and pleasing to God—this is your true and proper worship.

ROMANS 12:1

Therefore,
"Come out from them
and be separate,
says the Lord.
Touch no unclean thing,
and I will receive you."
And,
"I will be a Father to you,
and you will be my sons and daughters,
says the Lord Almighty."

2 CORINTHIANS 6:17–18

Since, then, you have been raised with Christ, set your hearts on things above, where Christ is, seated at the right hand of God. Set your minds on things above, not on earthly things.

COLOSSIANS 3:1–2

And whatever you do, whether in word or deed, do it all in the name of the Lord Jesus, giving thanks to God the Father through him.

COLOSSIANS 3:17

Make every effort to live in peace with everyone and to be holy; without holiness no one will see the Lord.

HEBREWS 12:14

But just as he who called you is holy, so be holy in all you do; for it is written: "Be holy, because I am holy."

1 PETER 1:15–16

As for other matters, brothers and sisters, we instructed you how to live in order to please God, as in fact you are living. Now we ask you and urge you in the Lord Jesus to do this more and more. For you know what instructions we gave you by the authority of the Lord Jesus. . . . For God did not call us to be impure, but to live a holy life.

1 THESSALONIANS 4:1–2, 7

THE HOLY SPIRIT

"And I will ask the Father, and he will give you another advocate to help you and be with you forever—the Spirit of truth. The world cannot accept him, because it neither sees him nor knows him. But you know him, for he lives with you and will be in you."

JOHN 14:16–17

"But when he, the Spirit of truth, comes, he will guide you into all the truth. He will not speak on his own; he will speak only what he hears, and he will tell you what is yet to come. He will glorify me because it is from me that he will receive what he will make known to you."

JOHN 16:13–14

"But you will receive power when the Holy Spirit comes on you; and you will be my witnesses in Jerusalem, and in all Judea and Samaria, and to the ends of the earth."

ACTS 1:8

For you were once darkness, but now you are light in the Lord. Live as children of light (for the fruit of the light consists in all goodness, righteousness and truth) and find out what pleases the Lord.

EPHESIANS 5:8–10

Since we live by the Spirit, let us keep in step with the Spirit.

GALATIANS 5:25

For those who are led by the Spirit of God are the children of God. The Spirit you received does not make you slaves, so that you live in fear again; rather, the Spirit you received brought about your adoption to sonship. And by him we cry, *"Abba,* Father." The Spirit himself testifies with our spirit that we are God's children.

ROMANS 8:14–16

But the fruit of the Spirit is love, joy, peace, forbearance, kindness, goodness, faithfulness, gentleness and self-control. Against such things there is no law.

GALATIANS 5:22–23

LEADING SOMEONE TO CHRIST

Once you were alienated from God and were enemies in your minds because of your evil behavior. But now he has reconciled you by Christ's physical body through death to present you holy in his sight, without blemish and free from accusation.

COLOSSIANS 1:21–22

For all have sinned and fall short of the glory of God, and all are justified freely by his grace through the redemption that came by Christ Jesus.

ROMANS 3:23–24

For the wages of sin is death, but the gift of God is eternal life in Christ Jesus our Lord.

ROMANS 6:23

"Just as Moses lifted up the snake in the wilderness, so the Son of Man must be lifted up, that everyone who believes may have eternal life in him.

"For God so loved the world that he gave his one and only Son, that whoever believes in him shall not perish but have eternal life."

JOHN 3:14–16

For it is by grace you have been saved, through faith—and this is not from yourselves, it is the gift of God—not by works, so that no one can boast.

EPHESIANS 2:8–9

But when the kindness and love of God our Savior appeared, he saved us, not because of righteous things we had done, but because of his mercy. He saved us through the washing of rebirth and renewal by the Holy Spirit, whom he poured out on us generously through Jesus Christ our Savior, so that, having been justified by his grace, we might become heirs having the hope of eternal life.

TITUS 3:4–7

Jesus answered, "I am the way and the truth and the life. No one comes to the Father except through me."

JOHN 14:6

If you declare with your mouth, "Jesus is Lord," and believe in your heart that God raised him from the dead, you will be saved. For it is with your heart that you believe and are justified, and it is with your mouth that you profess your faith and are saved.

ROMANS 10:9–10

LOVE OF GOD

But God demonstrates his own love for us in this: While we were still sinners, Christ died for us.

ROMANS 5:8

"No, the Father himself loves you because you have loved me and have believed that I came from God."

JOHN 16:27

For I am convinced that neither death nor life, neither angels nor demons, neither the present nor the future, nor any powers, neither height nor depth, nor anything else in all creation, will be able to separate us from the love of God that is in Christ Jesus our Lord.

ROMANS 8:38–39

But because of his great love for us, God, who is rich in mercy, made us alive with Christ even when we were dead in transgressions—it is by grace you have been saved.

EPHESIANS 2:4–5

I pray that out of his glorious riches he may strengthen you with power through his Spirit in your inner being so that Christ may dwell in your hearts through faith. And I pray that you, being rooted and established in love, may have power, together with all the Lord's holy people, to grasp how wide and long and high and deep is the love of Christ, and to know this love that surpasses knowledge—that you may be filled to the measure of all the fullness of God.

EPHESIANS 3:17–19

See what great love the Father has lavished on us, that we should be called children of God! And that is what we are! The reason the world does not know us is that it did not know him.

1 JOHN 3:1

"Greater love has no one than this: to lay down one's life for one's friends."

JOHN 15:13

This is love: not that we loved God, but that he loved us and sent his Son as an atoning sacrifice for our sins.

1 JOHN 4:10

"For God so loved the world that he gave his one and only Son, that whoever believes in him shall not perish but have eternal life."

JOHN 3:16

Jesus replied: "'Love the Lord your God with all your heart and with all your soul and with all your mind.' This is the first and greatest commandment. And the second is like it: 'Love your neighbor as yourself.'"

MATTHEW 22:37–39

Jesus replied, "Anyone who loves me will obey my teaching. My Father will love them, and we will come to them and make our home with them. Anyone who does not love me will not obey my teaching. These words you hear are not my own; they belong to the Father who sent me."

JOHN 14:23–24

LOVE OF OTHERS

Above all, love each other deeply, because love covers over a multitude of sins.

1 PETER 4:8

This is how we know what love is: Jesus Christ laid down his life for us. And we ought to lay down our lives for our brothers and sisters.

1 JOHN 3:16

Finally, all of you, be like-minded, be sympathetic, love one another, be compassionate and humble.

1 PETER 3:8

Love must be sincere. Hate what is evil; cling to what is good. Be devoted to one another in love. Honor one another above yourselves.

ROMANS 12:9–10

Now that you have purified yourselves by obeying the truth so that you have sincere love for each other, love one another deeply, from the heart.

1 PETER 1:22

Therefore, as we have opportunity, let us do good to all people, especially to those who belong to the family of believers.

GALATIANS 6:10

"Now that I, your Lord and Teacher, have washed your feet, you also should wash one another's feet. I have set you an example that you should do as I have done for you."

JOHN 13:14–15

And over all these virtues put on love, which binds them all together in perfect unity.

COLOSSIANS 3:14

Love is patient, love is kind. It does not envy, it does not boast, it is not proud.

1 CORINTHIANS 13:4

May the Lord make your love increase and overflow for each other and for everyone else, just as ours does for you.

1 THESSALONIANS 3:12

MARRIAGE

The Lord God said, "It is not good for the man to be alone. I will make a helper suitable for him."

Genesis 2:18

Two are better than one,
>   because they have a good return for their labor:
If either of them falls down,
>   one can help the other up.
But pity anyone who falls
>   and has no one to help them up.
Also, if two lie down together, they will keep warm.
>   But how can one keep warm alone?
Though one may be overpowered,
>   two can defend themselves.
A cord of three strands is not quickly broken.

Ecclesiastes 4:9–12

Love is patient, love is kind. It does not envy, it does not boast, it is not proud. It does not dishonor others, it is not self-seeking, it is not easily angered, it keeps no record of wrongs. Love does not delight in evil but rejoices with the truth. It always protects, always trusts, always hopes, always perseveres.

Love never fails. But where there are prophecies, they will cease; where there are tongues, they will be stilled; where there is knowledge, it will pass away.

1 Corinthians 13:4–8

He who finds a wife finds what is good
and receives favor from the LORD.

PROVERBS 18:22

"Haven't you read," he replied, "that at the beginning
the Creator 'made them male and female,' and said, 'For
this reason a man will leave his father and mother and
be united to his wife, and the two will become one flesh'?
So they are no longer two, but one flesh. Therefore what
God has joined together, let no one separate."

MATTHEW 19:4–6

Houses and wealth are inherited from parents,
but a prudent wife is from the LORD.

PROVERBS 19:14

May your fountain be blessed,
and may you rejoice in the wife of your youth.

PROVERBS 5:18

Be kind and compassionate to one another, forgiving
each other, just as in Christ God forgave you.

EPHESIANS 4:32

Do you not know that your bodies are temples of
the Holy Spirit, who is in you, whom you have received
from God? You are not your own; you were bought at a
price. Therefore honor God with your bodies.

1 CORINTHIANS 6:19–20

Wives, submit yourselves to your own husbands as you do to the Lord. For the husband is the head of the wife as Christ is the head of the church, his body, of which he is the Savior. Now as the church submits to Christ, so also wives should submit to their husbands in everything.

Husbands, love your wives, just as Christ loved the church and gave himself up for her to make her holy, cleansing her by the washing with water through the word, and to present her to himself as a radiant church, without stain or wrinkle or any other blemish, but holy and blameless. In this same way, husbands ought to love their wives as their own bodies. He who loves his wife loves himself. After all, no one ever hated their own body, but they feed and care for their body, just as Christ does the church—for we are members of his body. "For this reason a man will leave his father and mother and be united to his wife, and the two will become one flesh." This is a profound mystery—but I am talking about Christ and the church. However, each one of you also must love his wife as he loves himself, and the wife must respect her husband.

EPHESIANS 5:22–33

WHAT THE BIBLE HAS TO SAY ABOUT . . .
MONEY

"No one can serve two masters. Either you will hate the one and love the other, or you will be devoted to the one and despise the other. You cannot serve both God and money."

LUKE 16:13

For the love of money is a root of all kinds of evil. Some people, eager for money, have wandered from the faith and pierced themselves with many griefs.

1 TIMOTHY 6:10

"Bring the whole tithe into the storehouse, that there may be food in my house. Test me in this," says the LORD Almighty, "and see if I will not throw open the floodgates of heaven and pour out so much blessing that there will not be room enough to store it."

MALACHI 3:10

Give generously to them and do so without a grudging heart; then because of this the LORD your God will bless you in all your work and in everything you put your hand to.

DEUTERONOMY 15:10

A generous person will prosper;
   whoever refreshes others will be refreshed.

PROVERBS 11:25

Each of you should give what you have decided in your heart to give, not reluctantly or under compulsion, for God loves a cheerful giver.

2 CORINTHIANS 9:7

I am not saying this because I am in need, for I have learned to be content whatever the circumstances. I know what it is to be in need, and I know what it is to have plenty. I have learned the secret of being content in any and every situation, whether well fed or hungry, whether living in plenty or in want.

PHILIPPIANS 4:11–12

"Why spend money on what is not bread,
    and your labor on what does not satisfy?
Listen, listen to me, and eat what is good,
    and you will delight in the richest of fare."

ISAIAH 55:2

OBEDIENCE

Let everyone be subject to the governing authorities, for there is no authority except that which God has established. The authorities that exist have been established by God.

ROMANS 13:1

Children, obey your parents in everything, for this pleases the Lord.

COLOSSIANS 3:20

Remind the people to be subject to rulers and authorities, to be obedient, to be ready to do whatever is good, to slander no one, to be peaceable and considerate, and always to be gentle toward everyone.

TITUS 3:1–2

Submit yourselves for the Lord's sake to every human authority: whether to the emperor, as the supreme authority, or to governors, who are sent by him to punish those who do wrong and to commend those who do right.

1 PETER 2:13–14

Now if you obey me fully and keep my covenant, then out of all nations you will be my treasured possession.

EXODUS 19:5

Be diligent in these matters; give yourself wholly to them, so that everyone may see your progress.

1 TIMOTHY 4:15

"But I gave them this command: Obey me, and I will be your God and you will be my people. Walk in obedience to all I command you, that it may go well with you. But they did not listen or pay attention; instead, they followed the stubborn inclinations of their evil hearts. They went backward and not forward."

JEREMIAH 7:23–24

OVERCOMING EVIL

Do not repay anyone evil for evil. Be careful to do what is right in the eyes of everyone. If it is possible, as far as it depends on you, live at peace with everyone. Do not take revenge, my dear friends, but leave room for God's wrath, for it is written: "It is mine to avenge; I will repay," says the Lord. On the contrary:
"If your enemy is hungry, feed him;
    if he is thirsty, give him something to drink.
In doing this, you will heap burning coals on his
    head."

ROMANS 12:17–20

Finally, all of you, be like-minded, be sympathetic, love one another, be compassionate and humble. Do not repay evil with evil or insult with insult. On the contrary, repay evil with blessing, because to this you were called so that you may inherit a blessing.

1 PETER 3:8–9

You, dear children, are from God and have overcome them, because the one who is in you is greater than the one who is in the world.

1 JOHN 4:4

Dear friend, do not imitate what is evil but what is good. Anyone who does what is good is from God. Anyone who does what is evil has not seen God.

3 JOHN V.11

Do not say, "I'll pay you back for this wrong!"
    Wait for the LORD, and he will avenge you.

PROVERBS 20:22

Bless those who persecute you; bless and do not curse.

ROMANS 12:14

Even though I walk
    through the darkest valley,
I will fear no evil,
    for you are with me;
your rod and your staff,
    they comfort me.

PSALM 23:4

Turn from evil and do good;
    then you will dwell in the land forever.
For the LORD loves the just
    and will not forsake his faithful ones.
Wrongdoers will be completely destroyed;
    the offspring of the wicked will perish.

PSALM 37:27–28

Let those who love the LORD hate evil,
    for he guards the lives of his faithful ones
    and delivers them from the hand of the wicked.

PSALM 97:10

    Get rid of all bitterness, rage and anger, brawling and slander, along with every form of malice. Be kind and compassionate to one another, forgiving each other, just as in Christ God forgave you.

EPHESIANS 4:31–32

LORD, who may dwell in your sacred tent?
    Who may live on your holy mountain?
The one whose walk is blameless,
    who does what is righteous,
    who speaks the truth from their heart.

PSALM 15:1–2

Keep your tongue from evil
    and your lips from telling lies.
Turn from evil and do good;
    seek peace and pursue it.
The eyes of the LORD are on the righteous,
    and his ears are attentive to their cry.

PSALM 34:13–15

PATIENCE AND PERSEVERANCE

Be still before the LORD
    and wait patiently for him;
do not fret when people succeed in their ways,
    when they carry out their wicked schemes.

PSALM 37:7

I waited patiently for the LORD;
    he turned to me and heard my cry.

PSALM 40:1

Therefore we do not lose heart. Though outwardly we are wasting away, yet inwardly we are being renewed day by day. For our light and momentary troubles are achieving for us an eternal glory that far outweighs them all. So we fix our eyes not on what is seen, but on what is unseen, since what is seen is temporary, but what is unseen is eternal.

2 CORINTHIANS 4:16–18

Be patient, then, brothers and sisters, until the Lord's coming. See how the farmer waits for the land to yield its valuable crop, patiently waiting for the autumn and spring rains. You too, be patient and stand firm, because the Lord's coming is near.

JAMES 5:7–8

For this very reason, make every effort to add to your faith goodness; and to goodness, knowledge; and to knowledge, self-control; and to self-control, perseverance; and to perseverance, godliness; and to godliness, mutual affection; and to mutual affection, love. For if you possess these qualities in increasing measure, they will keep you from being ineffective and unproductive in your knowledge of our Lord Jesus Christ.

2 PETER 1:5–8

Consider it pure joy, my brothers and sisters, whenever you face trials of many kinds, because you know that the testing of your faith produces perseverance. Let perseverance finish its work so that you may be mature and complete, not lacking anything.

JAMES 1:2–4

The LORD is good to those whose hope is in him,
    to the one who seeks him;
it is good to wait quietly
    for the salvation of the LORD.
It is good for a man to bear the yoke
    while he is young.

LAMENTATIONS 3:25–27

May the God who gives endurance and encouragement give you the same attitude of mind toward each other that Christ Jesus had, so that with one mind and one voice you may glorify the God and Father of our Lord Jesus Christ.

ROMANS 15:5–6

However, I consider my life worth nothing to me; my only aim is to finish the race and complete the task the Lord Jesus has given me—the task of testifying to the good news of God's grace.

ACTS 20:24

The LORD is my rock, my fortress and my deliverer;
    my God is my rock, in whom I take refuge,
    my shield and the horn of my salvation, my
        stronghold.

PSALM 18:2

"Since you have kept my command to endure patiently, I will also keep you from the hour of trial that is going to come on the whole world to test the inhabitants of the earth."

REVELATION 3:10

PRAISE

Because your love is better than life,
    my lips will glorify you.
I will praise you as long as I live,
    and in your name I will lift up my hands.

PSALM 63:3–4

For great is the LORD and most worthy of praise;
    he is to be feared above all gods.

PSALM 96:4

Enter his gates with thanksgiving
    and his courts with praise;
    give thanks to him and praise his name.

PSALM 100:4

On the contrary, we speak as those approved by God to be entrusted with the gospel. We are not trying to please people but God, who tests our hearts.

1 THESSALONIANS 2:4

"In the same way, let your light shine before others, that they may see your good deeds and glorify your Father in heaven."

MATTHEW 5:16

"The people I formed for myself
that they may proclaim my praise."

ISAIAH 43:21

Through Jesus, therefore, let us continually offer to God a sacrifice of praise—the fruit of lips that openly profess his name.

HEBREWS 13:15

But you are a chosen people, a royal priesthood, a holy nation, God's special possession, that you may declare the praises of him who called you out of darkness into his wonderful light.

1 PETER 2:9

Therefore judge nothing before the appointed time; wait until the Lord comes. He will bring to light what is hidden in darkness and will expose the motives of the heart. At that time each will receive their praise from God.

1 CORINTHIANS 4:5

Praise the LORD.
How good it is to sing praises to our God,
how pleasant and fitting to praise him!

PSALM 147:1

I will praise the Lord all my life;
    I will sing praise to my God as long as I live. . . .
Blessed are those whose help is the God of Jacob,
    whose hope is in the Lord their God.

Psalm 146:2, 5

Praise the Lord.
Praise God in his sanctuary;
    praise him in his mighty heavens.
Praise him for his acts of power;
    praise him for his surpassing greatness.
Praise him with the sounding of the trumpet,
    praise him with the harp and lyre,
praise him with timbrel and dancing,
    praise him with the strings and pipe,
praise him with the clash of cymbals,
    praise him with resounding cymbals.
Let everything that has breath praise the Lord.
Praise the Lord.

Psalm 150:1–6

PRIDE

When pride comes, then comes disgrace,
    but with humility comes wisdom.

PROVERBS 11:2

Wisdom's instruction is to fear the LORD,
    and humility comes before honor.

PROVERBS 15:33

Pride brings a person low,
    but the lowly in spirit gain honor.

PROVERBS 29:23

This is what the LORD says:
    "Let not the wise boast of their wisdom
        or the strong boast of their strength
        or the rich boast of their riches,
    but let the one who boasts boast about this:
        that they have the understanding to know me,
    that I am the LORD, who exercises kindness,
        justice and righteousness on earth,
        for in these I delight,"
        declares the LORD.

JEREMIAH 9:23–24

"For all those who exalt themselves will be humbled,
and those who humble themselves will be exalted."

LUKE 14:11

I myself have reasons for such confidence. If someone else thinks they have reasons to put confidence in the flesh, I have more. . . . But whatever were gains to me I now consider loss for the sake of Christ. What is more, I consider everything a loss because of the surpassing worth of knowing Christ Jesus my Lord, for whose sake I have lost all things. I consider them garbage, that I may gain Christ.

PHILIPPIANS 3:4, 7–8

"Whoever wants to become great among you must be your servant, and whoever wants to be first must be your slave."

MATTHEW 20:26–27

For by the grace given me I say to every one of you: Do not think of yourself more highly than you ought, but rather think of yourself with sober judgment, in accordance with the faith God has distributed to each of you.

ROMANS 12:3

"Has not my hand made all these things,
    and so they came into being?"
        declares the LORD.
"These are the ones I look on with favor:
    those who are humble and contrite in spirit,
    and who tremble at my word."

ISAIAH 66:2

Where there is strife, there is pride,
 but wisdom is found in those who take advice.

PROVERBS 13:10

Do nothing out of selfish ambition or vain conceit. Rather, in humility value others above yourselves, not looking to your own interests but each of you to the interests of the others.

PHILIPPIANS 2:3–4

In the same way, you who are younger, submit yourselves to your elders. All of you, clothe yourselves with humility toward one another, because,
 "God opposes the proud
  but shows favor to the humble."

1 PETER 5:5

PURITY

Finally, brothers and sisters, whatever is true, whatever is noble, whatever is right, whatever is pure, whatever is lovely, whatever is admirable—if anything is excellent or praiseworthy—think about such things. Whatever you have learned or received or heard from me, or seen in me—put it into practice. And the God of peace will be with you.

PHILIPPIANS 4:8–9

So I say, walk by the Spirit, and you will not gratify the desires of the flesh.

GALATIANS 5:16

No temptation has overtaken you except what is common to mankind. And God is faithful; he will not let you be tempted beyond what you can bear. But when you are tempted, he will also provide a way out so that you can endure it.

1 CORINTHIANS 10:13

For the grace of God has appeared that offers salvation to all people. It teaches us to say "No" to ungodliness and worldly passions, and to live self-controlled, upright and godly lives in this present age.

TITUS 2:11–12

Put to death, therefore, whatever belongs to your earthly nature: sexual immorality, impurity, lust, evil desires and greed, which is idolatry.

COLOSSIANS 3:5

You were bought at a price. Therefore honor God with your bodies.

1 CORINTHIANS 6:20

Do not offer any part of yourself to sin as an instrument of wickedness, but rather offer yourselves to God as those who have been brought from death to life; and offer every part of yourself to him as an instrument of righteousness.

ROMANS 6:13

Through Christ Jesus the law of the Spirit who gives life has set you free from the law of sin and death.

ROMANS 8:2

SATAN

Finally, be strong in the Lord and in his mighty power. Put on the full armor of God, so that you can take your stand against the devil's schemes. For our struggle is not against flesh and blood, but against the rulers, against the authorities, against the powers of this dark world and against the spiritual forces of evil in the heavenly realms. Therefore put on the full armor of God, so that when the day of evil comes, you may be able to stand your ground, and after you have done everything, to stand.

EPHESIANS 6:10–13

Submit yourselves, then, to God. Resist the devil, and he will flee from you. Come near to God and he will come near to you. Wash your hands, you sinners, and purify your hearts, you double-minded.

JAMES 4:7–8

Be alert and of sober mind. Your enemy the devil prowls around like a roaring lion looking for someone to devour. Resist him, standing firm in the faith, because you know that the family of believers throughout the world is undergoing the same kind of sufferings.

1 PETER 5:8–9

The night is nearly over; the day is almost here. So let us put aside the deeds of darkness and put on the armor of light.

ROMANS 13:12

"I have told you these things, so that in me you may have peace. In this world you will have trouble. But take heart! I have overcome the world."

JOHN 16:33

Since, then, you have been raised with Christ, set your hearts on things above, where Christ is, seated at the right hand of God. Set your minds on things above, not on earthly things. For you died, and your life is now hidden with Christ in God.

COLOSSIANS 3:1–3

For though we live in the world, we do not wage war as the world does. The weapons we fight with are not the weapons of the world. On the contrary, they have divine power to demolish strongholds. We demolish arguments and every pretension that sets itself up against the knowledge of God, and we take captive every thought to make it obedient to Christ.

2 CORINTHIANS 10:3–5

SELF-CENTEREDNESS

Do nothing out of selfish ambition or vain conceit. Rather, in humility value others above yourselves, not looking to your own interests but each of you to the interests of the others.

PHILIPPIANS 2:3–4

Then he said to them all: "Whoever wants to be my disciple must deny themselves and take up their cross daily and follow me. For whoever wants to save their life will lose it, but whoever loses their life for me will save it. What good is it for someone to gain the whole world, and yet lose or forfeit their very self?"

LUKE 9:23–25

"By this everyone will know that you are my disciples, if you love one another."

JOHN 13:35

Be devoted to one another in love. Honor one another above yourselves.

ROMANS 12:10

Each of us should please our neighbors for their good, to build them up. For even Christ did not please himself but, as it is written: "The insults of those who insult you have fallen on me."

ROMANS 15:2–3

Carry each other's burdens, and in this way you will fulfill the law of Christ.

GALATIANS 6:2

"Whoever wants to become great among you must be your servant, and whoever wants to be first must be your slave—just as the Son of Man did not come to be served, but to serve, and to give his life as a ransom for many."

MATTHEW 20:26–28

No one should seek their own good, but the good of others.

1 CORINTHIANS 10:24

SELF-CONTROL

For this very reason, make every effort to add to your faith goodness; and to goodness, knowledge; and to knowledge, self-control; and to self-control, perseverance; and to perseverance, godliness.

2 PETER 1:5–6

You were taught to be made new in the attitude of your minds; and to put on the new self, created to be like God in true righteousness and holiness.

EPHESIANS 4:23–24

Fools give full vent to their rage,
    but the wise bring calm in the end.

PROVERBS 29:11

Everyone who competes in the games goes into strict training. They do it to get a crown that will not last, but we do it to get a crown that will last forever. Therefore I do not run like someone running aimlessly; I do not fight like a boxer beating the air. No, I strike a blow to my body and make it my slave so that after I have preached to others, I myself will not be disqualified for the prize.

1 CORINTHIANS 9:25–27

So then, let us not be like others, who are asleep, but let us be awake and sober. For those who sleep, sleep at night, and those who get drunk, get drunk at night. But since we belong to the day, let us be sober, putting on faith and love as a breastplate, and the hope of salvation as a helmet.

1 Thessalonians 5:6–8

But the fruit of the Spirit is love, joy, peace, forbearance, kindness, goodness, faithfulness, gentleness and self-control. Against such things there is no law. Those who belong to Christ Jesus have crucified the flesh with its passions and desires.

Galatians 5:22–24

SEX LIFE

"Blessed are the pure in heart,
    for they will see God."

MATTHEW 5:8

May your fountain be blessed,
    and may you rejoice in the wife of your youth.

PROVERBS 5:18

Do you not know that your bodies are members of Christ himself? Shall I then take the members of Christ and unite them with a prostitute? Never! Do you not know that he who unites himself with a prostitute is one with her in body? For it is said, "The two will become one flesh." But whoever is united with the Lord is one with him in spirit.

Flee from sexual immorality. All other sins a person commits are outside the body, but whoever sins sexually, sins against their own body. Do you not know that your bodies are temples of the Holy Spirit, who is in you, whom you have received from God? You are not your own; you were bought at a price. Therefore honor God with your bodies.

1 CORINTHIANS 6:15–20

But if we walk in the light, as he is in the light, we have fellowship with one another, and the blood of Jesus, his Son, purifies us from all sin.

1 John 1:7

It is God's will that you should be sanctified: that you should avoid sexual immorality; that each of you should learn to control your own body in a way that is holy and honorable, not in passionate lust like the pagans, who do not know God.

1 Thessalonians 4:3–5

Flee the evil desires of youth and pursue righteousness, faith, love and peace, along with those who call on the Lord out of a pure heart.

2 Timothy 2:22

Marriage should be honored by all, and the marriage bed kept pure, for God will judge the adulterer and all the sexually immoral.

Hebrews 13:4

Do not love the world or anything in the world. If anyone loves the world, love for the Father is not in them. For everything in the world—the lust of the flesh, the lust of the eyes, and the pride of life—comes not from the Father but from the world.

1 John 2:15–16

TEMPTATION

No temptation has overtaken you except what is common to mankind. And God is faithful; he will not let you be tempted beyond what you can bear. But when you are tempted, he will also provide a way out so that you can endure it.

1 CORINTHIANS 10:13

Because he himself suffered when he was tempted, he is able to help those who are being tempted.

HEBREWS 2:18

Finally, be strong in the Lord and in his mighty power. Put on the full armor of God, so that you can take your stand against the devil's schemes. For our struggle is not against flesh and blood, but against the rulers, against the authorities, against the powers of this dark world and against the spiritual forces of evil in the heavenly realms.

EPHESIANS 6:10–12

For we do not have a high priest who is unable to empathize with our weaknesses, but we have one who has been tempted in every way, just as we are—yet he did not sin. Let us then approach God's throne of grace with confidence, so that we may receive mercy and find grace to help us in our time of need.

HEBREWS 4:15–16

Blessed is the one who perseveres under trial because, having stood the test, that person will receive the crown of life that the Lord has promised to those who love him.

JAMES 1:12

"Watch and pray so that you will not fall into temptation. The spirit is willing, but the flesh is weak."

MATTHEW 26:41

Search me, God, and know my heart;
   test me and know my anxious thoughts.
See if there is any offensive way in me,
   and lead me in the way everlasting.

PSALM 139:23–24

"This, then, is how you should pray:
   "'Our Father in heaven,
   hallowed be your name . . .
   And lead us not into temptation,
      but deliver us from the evil one.'"

MATTHEW 6:9, 13

I have hidden your word in my heart
   that I might not sin against you.

PSALM 119:11

THANKFULNESS

Shout for joy to the LORD, all the earth.
Worship the LORD with gladness;
come before him with joyful songs.
Know that the LORD is God.
It is he who made us, and we are his;
we are his people, the sheep of his pasture.
Enter his gates with thanksgiving
and his courts with praise;
give thanks to him and praise his name.
For the LORD is good and his love endures forever;
his faithfulness continues through all generations.

PSALM 100:1–5

Give thanks in all circumstances; for this is God's will
for you in Christ Jesus.

1 THESSALONIANS 5:18

"Sacrifice thank offerings to God,
fulfill your vows to the Most High."

PSALM 50:14

Give praise to the LORD, proclaim his name;
make known among the nations what he has done.

PSALM 105:1

Be filled with the Spirit, speaking to one another with psalms, hymns, and songs from the Spirit. Sing and make music from your heart to the Lord, always giving thanks to God the Father for everything, in the name of our Lord Jesus Christ.

EPHESIANS 5:19–20

Let the peace of Christ rule in your hearts, since as members of one body you were called to peace. And be thankful.

COLOSSIANS 3:15

Through Jesus, therefore, let us continually offer to God a sacrifice of praise—the fruit of lips that openly profess his name.

HEBREWS 13:15

Whoever regards one day as special does so to the Lord. Whoever eats meat does so to the Lord, for they give thanks to God; and whoever abstains does so to the Lord and gives thanks to God.

ROMANS 14:6

But thanks be to God, who always leads us as captives in Christ's triumphal procession and uses us to spread the aroma of the knowledge of him everywhere.

2 CORINTHIANS 2:14

TRUST

Trust in the LORD with all your heart
　　and lean not on your own understanding;
in all your ways submit to him,
　　and he will make your paths straight.

PROVERBS 3:5–6

LORD Almighty,
　　blessed is the one who trusts in you.

PSALM 84:12

Do not put your trust in princes,
　　in human beings, who cannot save. . . .
Blessed are those whose help is the God of Jacob,
　　whose hope is in the LORD their God.

PSALM 146:3, 5

Trust in the LORD and do good;
　　dwell in the land and enjoy safe pasture.

PSALM 37:3

You will keep in perfect peace
　　those whose minds are steadfast,
　　because they trust in you.
Trust in the LORD forever,
　　for the LORD, the LORD himself, is the Rock
　　eternal.

ISAIAH 26:3–4

They will have no fear of bad news;
  their hearts are steadfast, trusting in the LORD.

PSALM 112:7

May your unfailing love come to me, LORD,
  your salvation, according to your promise;
then I can answer anyone who taunts me,
  for I trust in your word.

PSALM 119:41–42

The LORD is good,
  a refuge in times of trouble.
He cares for those who trust in him.

NAHUM 1:7

"Do not let your hearts be troubled. You believe in God; believe also in me."

JOHN 14:1

TRUTH

To the Jews who had believed him, Jesus said, "If you hold to my teaching, you are really my disciples. Then you will know the truth, and the truth will set you free."

JOHN 8:31–32

Jesus answered, "I am the way and the truth and the life. No one comes to the Father except through me."

JOHN 14:6

"When he, the Spirit of truth, comes, he will guide you into all the truth. He will not speak on his own; he will speak only what he hears, and he will tell you what is yet to come."

JOHN 16:13

Do your best to present yourself to God as one approved, a worker who does not need to be ashamed and who correctly handles the word of truth.

2 TIMOTHY 2:15

Your righteousness is everlasting
    and your law is true. . . .
All your words are true;
    all your righteous laws are eternal.

PSALM 119:142, 160

And you also were included in Christ when you heard the message of truth, the gospel of your salvation. When you believed, you were marked in him with a seal, the promised Holy Spirit.

EPHESIANS 1:13

Oh, how I love your law!
    I meditate on it all day long.
Your commands are always with me
    and make me wiser than my enemies.
I have more insight than all my teachers,
    for I meditate on your statutes.
I have more understanding than the elders,
    for I obey your precepts.

PSALM 119:97–100

UNPLANNED PREGNANCY

For you created my inmost being;
 you knit me together in my mother's womb.
I praise you because I am fearfully and wonderfully
 made;
 your works are wonderful,
 I know that full well.
My frame was not hidden from you
 when I was made in the secret place,
 when I was woven together in the depths of the
 earth.
Your eyes saw my unformed body;
 all the days ordained for me were written in your
 book
 before one of them came to be.

PSALM 139:13–16

The LORD is compassionate and gracious,
 slow to anger, abounding in love.
He will not always accuse,
 nor will he harbor his anger forever;
he does not treat us as our sins deserve
 or repay us according to our iniquities.
For as high as the heavens are above the earth,
 so great is his love for those who fear him;
as far as the east is from the west,
 so far has he removed our transgressions from us.

PSALM 103:8–12

And we know that in all things God works for the good of those who love him, who have been called according to his purpose.

ROMANS 8:28

Children are a heritage from the LORD,
    offspring a reward from him.

PSALM 127:3

But those who hope in the LORD
    will renew their strength.
They will soar on wings like eagles;
    they will run and not grow weary,
    they will walk and not be faint.

ISAIAH 40:31

"Before I formed you in the womb I knew you,
    before you were born I set you apart;
    I appointed you as a prophet to the nations."

JEREMIAH 1:5

Why, my soul, are you downcast?
    Why so disturbed within me?
Put your hope in God,
    for I will yet praise him,
    my Savior and my God.

PSALM 42:11

UNSELFISHNESS

Do nothing out of selfish ambition or vain conceit. Rather, in humility value others above yourselves, not looking to your own interests but each of you to the interests of the others.

PHILIPPIANS 2:3–4

Carry each other's burdens, and in this way you will fulfill the law of Christ.

GALATIANS 6:2

Whoever is kind to the poor lends to the LORD,
    and he will reward them for what they have done.

PROVERBS 19:17

Rejoice with those who rejoice; mourn with those who mourn. Live in harmony with one another. Do not be proud, but be willing to associate with people of low position. Do not be conceited.

ROMANS 12:15–16

Be devoted to one another in love. Honor one another above yourselves. . . . Share with the Lord's people who are in need. Practice hospitality.

ROMANS 12:10, 13

If you really keep the royal law found in Scripture,
"Love your neighbor as yourself," you are doing right.

JAMES 2:8

Follow God's example, therefore, as dearly loved
children and walk in the way of love, just as Christ loved
us and gave himself up for us as a fragrant offering and
sacrifice to God.

EPHESIANS 5:1–2

Give generously to them and do so without a
grudging heart; then because of this the LORD your God
will bless you in all your work and in everything you put
your hand to.

DEUTERONOMY 15:10

A generous person will prosper;
   whoever refreshes others will be refreshed.

PROVERBS 11:25

WHAT THE BIBLE HAS TO SAY ABOUT . . .
WORLDLINESS

Since, then, you have been raised with Christ, set your hearts on things above, where Christ is, seated at the right hand of God. Set your minds on things above, not on earthly things.

COLOSSIANS 3:1–2

Do not conform to the pattern of this world, but be transformed by the renewing of your mind. Then you will be able to test and approve what God's will is—his good, pleasing and perfect will.

ROMANS 12:2

For though we live in the world, we do not wage war as the world does. The weapons we fight with are not the weapons of the world. On the contrary, they have divine power to demolish strongholds.

2 CORINTHIANS 10:3–4

For the grace of God has appeared that offers salvation to all people. It teaches us to say "No" to ungodliness and worldly passions, and to live self-controlled, upright and godly lives in this present age, while we wait for the blessed hope—the appearing of the glory of our great God and Savior, Jesus Christ, who gave himself for us to redeem us from all wickedness and to purify for himself a people that are his very own, eager to do what is good.

TITUS 2:11–14

But our citizenship is in heaven. And we eagerly await a Savior from there, the Lord Jesus Christ, who, by the power that enables him to bring everything under his control, will transform our lowly bodies so that they will be like his glorious body.

Therefore, my brothers and sisters, you whom I love and long for, my joy and crown, stand firm in the Lord in this way, dear friends!

PHILIPPIANS 3:20–4:1

Dear friends, I urge you, as foreigners and exiles, to abstain from sinful desires, which wage war against your soul.

1 PETER 2:11

But God chose the foolish things of the world to shame the wise; God chose the weak things of the world to shame the strong.

1 CORINTHIANS 1:27

See what great love the Father has lavished on us, that we should be called children of God! And that is what we are! The reason the world does not know us is that it did not know him.

1 JOHN 3:1

WITNESSING

He said to them, "Go into all the world and preach the gospel to all creation."

MARK 16:15

He told them, "This is what is written: The Messiah will suffer and rise from the dead on the third day, and repentance for the forgiveness of sins will be preached in his name to all nations, beginning at Jerusalem."

LUKE 24:46–47

"But you will receive power when the Holy Spirit comes on you; and you will be my witnesses in Jerusalem, and in all Judea and Samaria, and to the ends of the earth."

ACTS 1:8

Then Jesus came to them and said, "All authority in heaven and on earth has been given to me. Therefore go and make disciples of all nations, baptizing them in the name of the Father and of the Son and of the Holy Spirit, and teaching them to obey everything I have commanded you. And surely I am with you always, to the very end of the age."

MATTHEW 28:18–20

"You are my witnesses," declares the LORD,
   "and my servant whom I have chosen,
so that you may know and believe me
   and understand that I am he.
Before me no god was formed,
   nor will there be one after me."

ISAIAH 43:10

For what we preach is not ourselves, but Jesus Christ as Lord, and ourselves as your servants for Jesus' sake. For God, who said, "Let light shine out of darkness," made his light shine in our hearts to give us the light of the knowledge of God's glory displayed in the face of Christ.

2 CORINTHIANS 4:5–6

WORK

And whatever you do, whether in word or deed, do it all in the name of the Lord Jesus, giving thanks to God the Father through him.

COLOSSIANS 3:17

Anyone who has been stealing must steal no longer, but must work, doing something useful with their own hands, that they may have something to share with those in need.

EPHESIANS 4:28

To make it your ambition to lead a quiet life: You should mind your own business and work with your hands, just as we told you, so that your daily life may win the respect of outsiders and so that you will not be dependent on anybody.

1 THESSALONIANS 4:11–12

May the favor of the Lord our God rest on us;
    establish the work of our hands for us—
    yes, establish the work of our hands.

PSALM 90:17

Such people we command and urge in the Lord Jesus Christ to settle down and earn the food they eat. And as for you, brothers and sisters, never tire of doing what is good.

2 Thessalonians 3:12–13

So whether you eat or drink or whatever you do, do it all for the glory of God.

1 Corinthians 10:31

Our people must learn to devote themselves to doing what is good, in order to provide for urgent needs and not live unproductive lives.

Titus 3:14

Whoever looks intently into the perfect law that gives freedom, and continues in it—not forgetting what they have heard, but doing it—they will be blessed in what they do.

James 1:25

YOUTH

Don't let anyone look down on you because you are young, but set an example for the believers in speech, in conduct, in love, in faith and in purity.

1 TIMOTHY 4:12

Since my youth, God, you have taught me,
    and to this day I declare your marvelous deeds.

PSALM 71:17

Listen, my son, to your father's instruction
    and do not forsake your mother's teaching.
They are a garland to grace your head
    and a chain to adorn your neck.

PROVERBS 1:8–9

Listen, my sons, to a father's instruction;
    pay attention and gain understanding.
I give you sound learning,
    so do not forsake my teaching.
For I too was a son to my father,
    still tender, and cherished by my mother.
Then he taught me, and he said to me,
    "Take hold of my words with all your heart;
    keep my commands, and you will live."

PROVERBS 4:1–4

The fear of the LORD is the beginning of wisdom,
 and knowledge of the Holy One is understanding.
For through wisdom your days will be many,
 and years will be added to your life.

PROVERBS 9:10–11

Whoever gives heed to instruction prospers,
 and blessed is the one who trusts in the LORD.

PROVERBS 16:20

"Honor your father and your mother, so that you may
live long in the land the LORD your God is giving you."

EXODUS 20:12

Children, obey your parents in the Lord, for this is
right. "Honor your father and mother"—which is the first
commandment with a promise—"so that it may go well
with you and that you may enjoy long life on the earth."

EPHESIANS 6:1–3

Children, obey your parents in everything, for this
pleases the Lord.

COLOSSIANS 3:20

In the same way, you who are younger, submit
yourselves to your elders. All of you, clothe yourselves
with humility toward one another, because,
 "God opposes the proud
 but shows favor to the humble."

1 PETER 5:5

WHAT JESUS MEANS TO YOU...

- His Death
- His Deity
- His Humanity
- His Resurrection
- His Second Coming
- His Love
- His Security
- His Fellowship

HIS DEATH

God made him who had no sin to be sin for us, so that in him we might become the righteousness of God.

2 CORINTHIANS 5:21

For Christ also suffered once for sins, the righteous for the unrighteous, to bring you to God. He was put to death in the body but made alive in the Spirit.

1 PETER 3:18

Later, knowing that everything had now been finished, and so that Scripture would be fulfilled, Jesus said, "I am thirsty." A jar of wine vinegar was there, so they soaked a sponge in it, put the sponge on a stalk of the hyssop plant, and lifted it to Jesus' lips. When he had received the drink, Jesus said, "It is finished." With that, he bowed his head and gave up his spirit.

JOHN 19:28–30

"He committed no sin,
    and no deceit was found in his mouth."
When they hurled their insults at him, he did not retaliate; when he suffered, he made no threats. Instead, he entrusted himself to him who judges justly. "He himself bore our sins" in his body on the cross, so that we might die to sins and live for righteousness; "by his wounds you have been healed."

1 PETER 2:22–24

You see, at just the right time, when we were still powerless, Christ died for the ungodly. Very rarely will anyone die for a righteous person, though for a good person someone might possibly dare to die. But God demonstrates his own love for us in this: While we were still sinners, Christ died for us.

ROMANS 5:6–8

He is the atoning sacrifice for our sins, and not only for ours but also for the sins of the whole world.

1 JOHN 2:2

WHAT JESUS MEANS TO YOU:
HIS DEITY

The Son is the image of the invisible God, the firstborn over all creation. For in him all things were created: things in heaven and on earth, visible and invisible, whether thrones or powers or rulers or authorities; all things have been created through him and for him. He is before all things, and in him all things hold together. And he is the head of the body, the church; he is the beginning and the firstborn from among the dead, so that in everything he might have the supremacy. For God was pleased to have all his fullness dwell in him, and through him to reconcile to himself all things, whether things on earth or things in heaven, by making peace through his blood, shed on the cross.

COLOSSIANS 1:15–20

In the beginning was the Word, and the Word was with God, and the Word was God. He was with God in the beginning. Through him all things were made; without him nothing was made that has been made.

JOHN 1:1–3

For us there is but one God, the Father, from whom all things came and for whom we live; and there is but one Lord, Jesus Christ, through whom all things came and through whom we live.

1 CORINTHIANS 8:6

"I give them eternal life, and they shall never perish; no one will snatch them out of my hand. My Father, who has given them to me, is greater than all; no one can snatch them out of my Father's hand. I and the Father are one."

JOHN 10:28–30

We wait for the blessed hope—the appearing of the glory of our great God and Savior, Jesus Christ.

TITUS 2:13

My dear children, I write this to you so that you will not sin. But if anybody does sin, we have an advocate with the Father—Jesus Christ, the Righteous One. He is the atoning sacrifice for our sins, and not only for ours but also for the sins of the whole world.

1 JOHN 2:1–2

Who is it that overcomes the world? Only the one who believes that Jesus is the Son of God.

1 JOHN 5:5

WHAT JESUS MEANS TO YOU:
HIS HUMANITY

But the angel said to her, "Do not be afraid, Mary; you have found favor with God. You will conceive and give birth to a son, and you are to call him Jesus. He will be great and will be called the Son of the Most High. The Lord God will give him the throne of his father David, and he will reign over Jacob's descendants forever; his kingdom will never end."

LUKE 1:30–33

Who, being in very nature God,
    did not consider equality with God something to
      be used to his own advantage;
rather, he made himself nothing
    by taking the very nature of a servant,
    being made in human likeness.
And being found in appearance as a man,
    he humbled himself
    by becoming obedient to death—
      even death on a cross!

PHILIPPIANS 2:6–8

Yet to all who did receive him, to those who believed in his name, he gave the right to become children of God.

JOHN 1:12

For we do not have a high priest who is unable to empathize with our weaknesses, but we have one who has been tempted in every way, just as we are—yet he did not sin."

HEBREWS 4:15

The Word became flesh and made his dwelling among us. We have seen his glory, the glory of the one and only Son, who came from the Father, full of grace and truth.

JOHN 1:14

But when the set time had fully come, God sent his Son, born of a woman, born under the law, to redeem those under the law, that we might receive adoption to sonship.

GALATIANS 4:4–5

WHAT JESUS MEANS TO YOU:
HIS RESURRECTION

Because Jesus lives forever, he has a permanent priesthood. Therefore he is able to save completely those who come to God through him, because he always lives to intercede for them.

HEBREWS 7:24–25

For what I received I passed on to you as of first importance: that Christ died for our sins according to the Scriptures, that he was buried, that he was raised on the third day according to the Scriptures, and that he appeared to Cephas, and then to the Twelve. After that, he appeared to more than five hundred of the brothers and sisters at the same time, most of whom are still living, though some have fallen asleep. Then he appeared to James, then to all the apostles, and last of all he appeared to me also, as to one abnormally born.

1 CORINTHIANS 15:3–8

And he is the head of the body, the church; he is the beginning and the firstborn from among the dead, so that in everything he might have the supremacy.

COLOSSIANS 1:18

The angel said to the women, "Do not be afraid, for I know that you are looking for Jesus, who was crucified. He is not here; he has risen, just as he said. Come and see the place where he lay."

MATTHEW 28:5–6

After he said this, he was taken up before their very eyes, and a cloud hid him from their sight.

ACTS 1:9

"I am the Living One; I was dead, and now look, I am alive for ever and ever! And I hold the keys of death and Hades."

REVELATION 1:18

WHAT JESUS MEANS TO YOU:
HIS SECOND COMING

For the Lord himself will come down from heaven, with a loud command, with the voice of the archangel and with the trumpet call of God, and the dead in Christ will rise first. After that, we who are still alive and are left will be caught up together with them in the clouds to meet the Lord in the air. And so we will be with the Lord forever. Therefore encourage one another with these words.

1 Thessalonians 4:16–18

"My Father's house has many rooms; if that were not so, would I have told you that I am going there to prepare a place for you? And if I go and prepare a place for you, I will come back and take you to be with me that you also may be where I am."

John 14:2–3

"So you also must be ready, because the Son of Man will come at an hour when you do not expect him."

Matthew 24:44

But do not forget this one thing, dear friends: With the Lord a day is like a thousand years, and a thousand years are like a day. The Lord is not slow in keeping his promise, as some understand slowness. Instead he is patient with you, not wanting anyone to perish, but everyone to come to repentance.

2 Peter 3:8–9

You are all children of the light and children of the day. We do not belong to the night or to the darkness. So then, let us not be like others, who are asleep, but let us be awake and sober.

1 THESSALONIANS 5:5–6

They were looking intently up into the sky as he was going, when suddenly two men dressed in white stood beside them. "Men of Galilee," they said, "why do you stand here looking into the sky? This same Jesus, who has been taken from you into heaven, will come back in the same way you have seen him go into heaven."

ACTS 1:10–11

WHAT JESUS MEANS TO YOU:
HIS LOVE

But God demonstrates his own love for us in this: While we were still sinners, Christ died for us.

ROMANS 5:8

"For God so loved the world that he gave his one and only Son, that whoever believes in him shall not perish but have eternal life."

JOHN 3:16

Dear friends, let us love one another, for love comes from God. Everyone who loves has been born of God and knows God. Whoever does not love does not know God, because God is love. This is how God showed his love among us: He sent his one and only Son into the world that we might live through him. This is love: not that we loved God, but that he loved us and sent his Son as an atoning sacrifice for our sins. Dear friends, since God so loved us, we also ought to love one another. No one has ever seen God; but if we love one another, God lives in us and his love is made complete in us.

1 JOHN 4:7–12

And so we know and rely on the love God has for us. God is love. Whoever lives in love lives in God, and God in them. . . . We love because he first loved us.

1 JOHN 4:16, 19

"As the Father has loved me, so have I loved you. Now remain in my love. If you keep my commands, you will remain in my love, just as I have kept my Father's commands and remain in his love. I have told you this so that my joy may be in you and that your joy may be complete. My command is this: Love each other as I have loved you. Greater love has no one than this: to lay down one's life for one's friends."

JOHN 15:9–13

So that Christ may dwell in your hearts through faith. And I pray that you, being rooted and established in love, may have power, together with all the Lord's holy people, to grasp how wide and long and high and deep is the love of Christ, and to know this love that surpasses knowledge—that you may be filled to the measure of all the fullness of God.

EPHESIANS 3:17–19

I love those who love me,
    and those who seek me find me.

PROVERBS 8:17

"Whoever has my commands and keeps them is the one who loves me. The one who loves me will be loved by my Father, and I too will love them and show myself to them."

JOHN 14:21

It was just before the Passover Festival. Jesus knew that the hour had come for him to leave this world and go to the Father. Having loved his own who were in the world, he loved them to the end.

JOHN 13:1

For I am convinced that neither death nor life, neither angels nor demons, neither the present nor the future, nor any powers, neither height nor depth, nor anything else in all creation, will be able to separate us from the love of God that is in Christ Jesus our Lord.

ROMANS 8:38–39

WHAT JESUS MEANS TO YOU:
HIS SECURITY

Praise be to the God and Father of our Lord Jesus Christ! In his great mercy he has given us new birth into a living hope through the resurrection of Jesus Christ from the dead, and into an inheritance that can never perish, spoil or fade. This inheritance is kept in heaven for you, who through faith are shielded by God's power until the coming of the salvation that is ready to be revealed in the last time.

1 PETER 1:3–5

"My sheep listen to my voice; I know them, and they follow me. I give them eternal life, and they shall never perish; no one will snatch them out of my hand. My Father, who has given them to me, is greater than all; no one can snatch them out of my Father's hand. I and the Father are one."

JOHN 10:27–30

In all my prayers for all of you, I always pray with joy because of your partnership in the gospel from the first day until now, being confident of this, that he who began a good work in you will carry it on to completion until the day of Christ Jesus.

PHILIPPIANS 1:4–6

But the Lord is faithful, and he will strengthen you and protect you from the evil one.

2 THESSALONIANS 3:3

To him who is able to keep you from stumbling and to present you before his glorious presence without fault and with great joy—to the only God our Savior be glory, majesty, power and authority, through Jesus Christ our Lord, before all ages, now and forevermore! Amen.

JUDE VV. 24–25

Lift up your eyes and look to the heavens:
    Who created all these?
He who brings out the starry host one by one
    and calls forth each of them by name.
Because of his great power and mighty strength,
    not one of them is missing.

ISAIAH 40:26

"Do not work for food that spoils, but for food that endures to eternal life, which the Son of Man will give you. For on him God the Father has placed his seal of approval."

JOHN 6:27

Now to him who is able to establish you in accordance with my gospel, the message I proclaim about Jesus Christ, in keeping with the revelation of the mystery hidden for long ages past . . . to the only wise God be glory forever through Jesus Christ! Amen.

ROMANS 16:25, 27

And you also were included in Christ when you heard the message of truth, the gospel of your salvation. When you believed, you were marked in him with a seal, the promised Holy Spirit, who is a deposit guaranteeing our inheritance until the redemption of those who are God's possession—to the praise of his glory.

EPHESIANS 1:13–14

Now it is God who makes both us and you stand firm in Christ. He anointed us, set his seal of ownership on us, and put his Spirit in our hearts as a deposit, guaranteeing what is to come.

2 CORINTHIANS 1:21–22

WHAT JESUS MEANS TO YOU:
HIS FELLOWSHIP

We proclaim to you what we have seen and heard, so that you also may have fellowship with us. And our fellowship is with the Father and with his Son, Jesus Christ.

1 JOHN 1:3

God is faithful, who has called you into fellowship with his Son, Jesus Christ our Lord.

1 CORINTHIANS 1:9

"Here I am! I stand at the door and knock. If anyone hears my voice and opens the door, I will come in and eat with that person, and they with me."

REVELATION 3:20

Jesus replied, "Anyone who loves me will obey my teaching. My Father will love them, and we will come to them and make our home with them."

JOHN 14:23

"Whoever has my commands and keeps them is the one who loves me. The one who loves me will be loved by my Father, and I too will love them and show myself to them."

JOHN 14:21

"For where two or three gather in my name, there am I with them."

MATTHEW 18:20

"Remain in me, as I also remain in you. No branch can bear fruit by itself; it must remain in the vine. Neither can you bear fruit unless you remain in me.

"I am the vine; you are the branches. If you remain in me and I in you, you will bear much fruit; apart from me you can do nothing. . . . If you remain in me and my words remain in you, ask whatever you wish, and it will be done for you."

JOHN 15:4–5, 7

Walk in the way of love, just as Christ loved us and gave himself up for us as a fragrant offering and sacrifice to God. . . . Speaking to one another with psalms, hymns, and songs from the Spirit. Sing and make music from your heart to the Lord . . . for we are members of his body.

EPHESIANS 5:2, 19, 30

This is the message we have heard from him and declare to you: God is light; in him there is no darkness at all. If we claim to have fellowship with him and yet walk in the darkness, we lie and do not live out the truth. But if we walk in the light, as he is in the light, we have fellowship with one another, and the blood of Jesus, his Son, purifies us from all sin.

1 JOHN 1:5–7

WHAT TO DO WHEN YOU ARE...

- Afraid
- Developing Bad Habits
- Lying
- In Need of Prayer
- Seeking God's Will
- Suffering
- Doubting Yourself
- Making Bad Choices
- Uncertain About God
- Totally Down

WHAT TO DO WHEN YOU ARE . . .

AFRAID

For the Spirit God gave us does not make us timid,
but gives us power, love and self-discipline.

2 TIMOTHY 1:7

The Spirit you received does not make you slaves, so
that you live in fear again; rather, the Spirit you received
brought about your adoption to sonship. And by him
we cry, *"Abba*, Father." The Spirit himself testifies with
our spirit that we are God's children.

ROMANS 8:15–16

In peace I will lie down and sleep,
>   for you alone, LORD,
>   make me dwell in safety.

PSALM 4:8

Whoever dwells in the shelter of the Most High
>   will rest in the shadow of the Almighty.
I will say of the LORD, "He is my refuge and my
>   fortress,
>   my God, in whom I trust."

PSALM 91:1–2

But those who hope in the Lord
    will renew their strength.
They will soar on wings like eagles;
    they will run and not grow weary,
        they will walk and not be faint.

ISAIAH 40:31

So we say with confidence,
    "The Lord is my helper; I will not be afraid.
        What can mere mortals do to me?"

HEBREWS 13:6

Even though I walk
    through the darkest valley,
I will fear no evil,
    for you are with me;
your rod and your staff,
    they comfort me.
You prepare a table before me
    in the presence of my enemies.
You anoint my head with oil;
    my cup overflows.

PSALM 23:4–5

The LORD is my light and my salvation—
    whom shall I fear?
The LORD is the stronghold of my life—
    of whom shall I be afraid? . . .
Though an army besiege me,
    my heart will not fear;
though war break out against me,
    even then I will be confident.

PSALM 27:1, 3

There is no fear in love. But perfect love drives out fear, because fear has to do with punishment. The one who fears is not made perfect in love.

1 JOHN 4:18

DEVELOPING BAD HABITS

Finally, brothers and sisters, whatever is true, whatever is noble, whatever is right, whatever is pure, whatever is lovely, whatever is admirable—if anything is excellent or praiseworthy—think about such things. Whatever you have learned or received or heard from me, or seen in me—put it into practice. And the God of peace will be with you.

PHILIPPIANS 4:8–9

I can do all this through him who gives me strength.

PHILIPPIANS 4:13

I have hidden your word in my heart
    that I might not sin against you.

PSALM 119:11

Submit yourselves, then, to God. Resist the devil, and he will flee from you. Come near to God and he will come near to you. Wash your hands, you sinners, and purify your hearts, you double-minded.

JAMES 4:7–8

May our Lord Jesus Christ himself and God our Father, who loved us and by his grace gave us eternal encouragement and good hope, encourage your hearts and strengthen you in every good deed and word.

2 THESSALONIANS 2:16–17

Therefore, I urge you, brothers and sisters, in view of God's mercy, to offer your bodies as a living sacrifice, holy and pleasing to God—this is your true and proper worship. Do not conform to the pattern of this world, but be transformed by the renewing of your mind. Then you will be able to test and approve what God's will is— his good, pleasing and perfect will.

ROMANS 12:1–2

Then he said to them all: "Whoever wants to be my disciple must deny themselves and take up their cross daily and follow me."

LUKE 9:23

I have been crucified with Christ and I no longer live, but Christ lives in me. The life I now live in the body, I live by faith in the Son of God, who loved me and gave himself for me.

GALATIANS 2:20

Do your best to present yourself to God as one approved, a worker who does not need to be ashamed and who correctly handles the word of truth.

2 TIMOTHY 2:15

LYING

Wash away all my iniquity
    and cleanse me from my sin. . . .
Yet you desired faithfulness even in the womb;
    you taught me wisdom in that secret place.

PSALM 51:2, 6

"These are the things you are to do: Speak the truth to each other, and render true and sound judgment in your courts; do not plot evil against each other, and do not love to swear falsely. I hate all this," declares the LORD.

ZECHARIAH 8:16–17

The LORD detests lying lips,
    but he delights in people who are trustworthy.

PROVERBS 12:22

Do not lie to each other, since you have taken off your old self with its practices.

COLOSSIANS 3:9

"All you need to say is simply 'Yes' or 'No'; anything beyond this comes from the evil one."

MATTHEW 5:37

Whoever of you loves life
    and desires to see many good days,
keep your tongue from evil
    and your lips from telling lies.

PSALM 34:12–13

May these words of my mouth and this meditation of
    my heart
        be pleasing in your sight,
        LORD, my Rock and my Redeemer.

PSALM 19:14

Let us therefore make every effort to do what leads to
peace and to mutual edification.

ROMANS 14:19

Make every effort to live in peace with everyone and
to be holy; without holiness no one will see the Lord.

HEBREWS 12:14

IN NEED OF PRAYER

Do not be anxious about anything, but in every situation, by prayer and petition, with thanksgiving, present your requests to God. And the peace of God, which transcends all understanding, will guard your hearts and your minds in Christ Jesus.

PHILIPPIANS 4:6–7

"Ask and it will be given to you; seek and you will find; knock and the door will be opened to you. For everyone who asks receives; the one who seeks finds; and to the one who knocks, the door will be opened."

MATTHEW 7:7–8

Therefore confess your sins to each other and pray for each other so that you may be healed. The prayer of a righteous person is powerful and effective.

JAMES 5:16

And pray in the Spirit on all occasions with all kinds of prayers and requests. With this in mind, be alert and always keep on praying for all the Lord's people.

EPHESIANS 6:18

This is the confidence we have in approaching God: that if we ask anything according to his will, he hears us.

1 JOHN 5:14

I cried out to him with my mouth;
  his praise was on my tongue.
If I had cherished sin in my heart,
  the Lord would not have listened;
but God has surely listened
  and has heard my prayer.
Praise be to God,
  who has not rejected my prayer
  or withheld his love from me!

PSALM 66:17–20

"Call to me and I will answer you and tell you great and unsearchable things you do not know."

JEREMIAH 33:3

SEEKING GOD'S WILL

Do not conform to the pattern of this world, but be transformed by the renewing of your mind. Then you will be able to test and approve what God's will is—his good, pleasing and perfect will.

ROMANS 12:2

In their hearts humans plan their course,
  but the LORD establishes their steps.

PROVERBS 16:9

Trust in the LORD with all your heart
  and lean not on your own understanding;
in all your ways submit to him,
  and he will make your paths straight.

PROVERBS 3:5–6

Your word is a lamp for my feet,
  a light on my path.

PSALM 119:105

Take delight in the LORD,
  and he will give you the desires of your heart.

PSALM 37:4

The LORD makes firm the steps
  of the one who delights in him.

PSALM 37:23

I will instruct you and teach you in the way you
  should go;
    I will counsel you with my loving eye on you.

PSALM 32:8

"For I know the plans I have for you," declares the
LORD, "plans to prosper you and not to harm you,
plans to give you hope and a future. Then you will call
on me and come and pray to me, and I will listen to you.
You will seek me and find me when you seek me with all
your heart."

JEREMIAH 29:11–13

All the ways of the LORD are loving and faithful
  toward those who keep the demands of his
    covenant.

PSALM 25:10

SUFFERING

Consider it pure joy, my brothers and sisters, whenever you face trials of many kinds, because you know that the testing of your faith produces perseverance. Let perseverance finish its work so that you may be mature and complete, not lacking anything.

JAMES 1:2–4

Dear friends, do not be surprised at the fiery ordeal that has come on you to test you, as though something strange were happening to you. But rejoice inasmuch as you participate in the sufferings of Christ, so that you may be overjoyed when his glory is revealed.

1 PETER 4:12–13

For our light and momentary troubles are achieving for us an eternal glory that far outweighs them all.

2 CORINTHIANS 4:17

The Spirit himself testifies with our spirit that we are God's children. Now if we are children, then we are heirs—heirs of God and co-heirs with Christ, if indeed we share in his sufferings in order that we may also share in his glory.

I consider that our present sufferings are not worth comparing with the glory that will be revealed in us.

ROMANS 8:16–18

Not only so, but we also glory in our sufferings, because we know that suffering produces perseverance; perseverance, character; and character, hope. And hope does not put us to shame, because God's love has been poured out into our hearts through the Holy Spirit, who has been given to us.

ROMANS 5:3–5

Is anyone among you in trouble? Let them pray. Is anyone happy? Let them sing songs of praise. Is anyone among you sick? Let them call the elders of the church to pray over them and anoint them with oil in the name of the Lord.

JAMES 5:13–14

But thanks be to God! He gives us the victory through our Lord Jesus Christ.

Therefore, my dear brothers and sisters, stand firm. Let nothing move you. Always give yourselves fully to the work of the Lord, because you know that your labor in the Lord is not in vain.

1 CORINTHIANS 15:57–58

"Call on me in the day of trouble;
I will deliver you, and you will honor me."

PSALM 50:15

DOUBTING YOURSELF

"So do not fear, for I am with you;
    do not be dismayed, for I am your God.
I will strengthen you and help you;
    I will uphold you with my righteous right hand."

ISAIAH 41:10

Because the Sovereign LORD helps me,
    I will not be disgraced.
Therefore have I set my face like flint,
    and I know I will not be put to shame.

ISAIAH 50:7

Cast your cares on the LORD
    and he will sustain you;
he will never let
    the righteous be shaken.

PSALM 55:22

For we are God's handiwork, created in Christ Jesus to do good works, which God prepared in advance for us to do.

EPHESIANS 2:10

For God is not a God of disorder but of peace—as in all the congregations of the Lord's people.

1 CORINTHIANS 14:33

For in Scripture it says:
"See, I lay a stone in Zion,
    a chosen and precious cornerstone,
and the one who trusts in him
    will never be put to shame."

1 PETER 2:6

"When you pass through the waters,
    I will be with you;
and when you pass through the rivers,
    they will not sweep over you.
When you walk through the fire,
    you will not be burned;
    the flames will not set you ablaze."

ISAIAH 43:2

Now may the God of peace, who through the blood
of the eternal covenant brought back from the dead
our Lord Jesus, that great Shepherd of the sheep, equip
you with everything good for doing his will, and may he
work in us what is pleasing to him, through Jesus Christ,
to whom be glory for ever and ever. Amen.

HEBREWS 13:20–21

For I am convinced that neither death nor life, neither
angels nor demons, neither the present nor the future,
nor any powers, neither height nor depth, nor anything
else in all creation, will be able to separate us from the
love of God that is in Christ Jesus our Lord.

ROMANS 8:38–39

WHAT TO DO WHEN YOU ARE . . .
MAKING BAD CHOICES

If we confess our sins, he is faithful and just and will forgive us our sins and purify us from all unrighteousness. If we claim we have not sinned, we make him out to be a liar and his word is not in us.

1 JOHN 1:9–10

So be careful to do what the LORD your God has commanded you; do not turn aside to the right or to the left. Walk in obedience to all that the LORD your God has commanded you, so that you may live and prosper and prolong your days in the land that you will possess.

DEUTERONOMY 5:32–33

Do not conform to the pattern of this world, but be transformed by the renewing of your mind. Then you will be able to test and approve what God's will is—his good, pleasing and perfect will.

ROMANS 12:2

"I will heal their waywardness
    and love them freely,
        for my anger has turned away from them."

HOSEA 14:4

The path of the righteous is level;
    you, the Upright One, make the way of the
    righteous smooth.

ISAIAH 26:7

May integrity and uprightness protect me,
    because my hope, LORD, is in you.

PSALM 25:21

Therefore, since we are surrounded by such a great
cloud of witnesses, let us throw off everything that
hinders and the sin that so easily entangles. And let us
run with perseverance the race marked out for us.

HEBREWS 12:1

When the LORD takes pleasure in anyone's way,
    he causes their enemies to make peace with them.
Better a little with righteousness
    than much gain with injustice.

PROVERBS 16:7–8

Let us not become weary in doing good, for at the
proper time we will reap a harvest if we do not give up.

GALATIANS 6:9

UNCERTAIN ABOUT GOD

"Have faith in God," Jesus answered. "Truly I tell you, if anyone says to this mountain, 'Go, throw yourself into the sea,' and does not doubt in their heart but believes that what they say will happen, it will be done for them. Therefore I tell you, whatever you ask for in prayer, believe that you have received it, and it will be yours."

MARK 11:22–24

"And do not set your heart on what you will eat or drink; do not worry about it. For the pagan world runs after all such things, and your Father knows that you need them. But seek his kingdom, and these things will be given to you as well."

LUKE 12:29–31

"As the rain and the snow
    come down from heaven,
and do not return to it
    without watering the earth
and making it bud and flourish,
    so that it yields seed for the sower and bread for
        the eater,
so is my word that goes out from my mouth:
    It will not return to me empty,
but will accomplish what I desire
    and achieve the purpose for which I sent it."

ISAIAH 55:10–11

"Remember the former things, those of long ago;
   I am God, and there is no other;
   I am God, and there is none like me.
I make known the end from the beginning,
   from ancient times, what is still to come.
I say, 'My purpose will stand,
   and I will do all that I please.'"

ISAIAH 46:9–10

May God himself, the God of peace, sanctify you through and through. May your whole spirit, soul and body be kept blameless at the coming of our Lord Jesus Christ. The one who calls you is faithful, and he will do it.

1 THESSALONIANS 5:23–24

The Lord is not slow in keeping his promise, as some understand slowness. Instead he is patient with you, not wanting anyone to perish, but everyone to come to repentance.

2 PETER 3:9

"Though the mountains be shaken
   and the hills be removed,
yet my unfailing love for you will not be shaken
   nor my covenant of peace be removed,"
   says the LORD, who has compassion on you.

ISAIAH 54:10

And we know that in all things God works for the good of those who love him, who have been called according to his purpose.

ROMANS 8:28

TOTALLY DOWN

You will keep in perfect peace
    those whose minds are steadfast,
    because they trust in you.
Trust in the LORD forever,
    for the LORD, the LORD himself, is the Rock
    eternal.

ISAIAH 26:3–4

And if the Spirit of him who raised Jesus from the dead is living in you, he who raised Christ from the dead will also give life to your mortal bodies because of his Spirit who lives in you.

ROMANS 8:11

Therefore, since we have been justified through faith, we have peace with God through our Lord Jesus Christ, through whom we have gained access by faith into this grace in which we now stand. And we boast in the hope of the glory of God.

ROMANS 5:1–2

For God, who said, "Let light shine out of darkness," made his light shine in our hearts to give us the light of the knowledge of God's glory displayed in the face of Christ. . . .

We are hard pressed on every side, but not crushed; perplexed, but not in despair; persecuted, but not abandoned; struck down, but not destroyed.

2 CORINTHIANS 4:6, 8–9

He will swallow up death forever.
The Sovereign LORD will wipe away the tears
    from all faces;
he will remove his people's disgrace
    from all the earth.
        The LORD has spoken.
In that day they will say,
  "Surely this is our God;
    we trusted in him, and he saved us.
This is the LORD, we trusted in him;
    let us rejoice and be glad in his salvation."

ISAIAH 25:8–9

The salvation of the righteous comes from the LORD;
    he is their stronghold in time of trouble.
The LORD helps them and delivers them;
    he delivers them from the wicked and saves them,
    because they take refuge in him.

PSALM 37:39–40

"Peace I leave with you; my peace I give you. I do not give to you as the world gives. Do not let your hearts be troubled and do not be afraid."

JOHN 14:27

May the God of hope fill you with all joy and peace as you trust in him, so that you may overflow with hope by the power of the Holy Spirit.

ROMANS 15:13

TRUTH FROM THE BIBLE ABOUT...

- Christian Fellowship
- Your Responsibility
- God's Will for Your Life
- Answered Prayer
- Speaking God's Word
- Forgiving Others
- God's Plan of Salvation

TRUTH FROM THE BIBLE ABOUT . . .

CHRISTIAN FELLOWSHIP

We proclaim to you what we have seen and heard, so that you also may have fellowship with us. And our fellowship is with the Father and with his Son, Jesus Christ. . . .

But if we walk in the light, as he is in the light, we have fellowship with one another, and the blood of Jesus, his Son, purifies us from all sin.

1 JOHN 1:3, 7

Walk in the way of love, just as Christ loved us and gave himself up for us as a fragrant offering and sacrifice to God. . . . Speaking to one another with psalms, hymns, and songs from the Spirit. Sing and make music from your heart to the Lord, always giving thanks to God the Father for everything, in the name of our Lord Jesus Christ.

EPHESIANS 5:2, 19–20

Consequently, you are no longer foreigners and strangers, but fellow citizens with God's people and also members of his household, built on the foundation of the apostles and prophets, with Christ Jesus himself as the chief cornerstone. In him the whole building is joined together and rises to become a holy temple in the Lord. And in him you too are being built together to become a dwelling in which God lives by his Spirit.

EPHESIANS 2:19–22

Let the message of Christ dwell among you richly as you teach and admonish one another with all wisdom through psalms, hymns, and songs from the Spirit, singing to God with gratitude in your hearts. And whatever you do, whether in word or deed, do it all in the name of the Lord Jesus, giving thanks to God the Father through him.

COLOSSIANS 3:16–17

My goal is that they may be encouraged in heart and united in love, so that they may have the full riches of complete understanding, in order that they may know the mystery of God, namely, Christ.

COLOSSIANS 2:2

For you are a people holy to the LORD your God. The LORD your God has chosen you out of all the peoples on the face of the earth to be his people, his treasured possession.

DEUTERONOMY 7:6

Therefore if you have any encouragement from being united with Christ, if any comfort from his love, if any common sharing in the Spirit, if any tenderness and compassion, then make my joy complete by being like-minded, having the same love, being one in spirit and of one mind.

PHILIPPIANS 2:1–2

I appeal to you, brothers and sisters, in the name of our Lord Jesus Christ, that all of you agree with one another in what you say and that there be no divisions among you, but that you be perfectly united in mind and thought.

1 CORINTHIANS 1:10

May the God who gives endurance and encouragement give you the same attitude of mind toward each other that Christ Jesus had, so that with one mind and one voice you may glorify the God and Father of our Lord Jesus Christ.

Accept one another, then, just as Christ accepted you, in order to bring praise to God.

ROMANS 15:5–7

Let us draw near to God with a sincere heart and with the full assurance that faith brings, having our hearts sprinkled to cleanse us from a guilty conscience and having our bodies washed with pure water. Let us hold unswervingly to the hope we profess, for he who promised is faithful. And let us consider how we may spur one another on toward love and good deeds, not giving up meeting together, as some are in the habit of doing, but encouraging one another—and all the more as you see the Day approaching.

HEBREWS 10:22–25

TRUTH FROM THE BIBLE ABOUT . . .
YOUR RESPONSIBILITY

"But you will receive power when the Holy Spirit comes on you; and you will be my witnesses in Jerusalem, and in all Judea and Samaria, and to the ends of the earth."

ACTS 1:8

"You are the light of the world. A town built on a hill cannot be hidden. Neither do people light a lamp and put it under a bowl. Instead they put it on its stand, and it gives light to everyone in the house. In the same way, let your light shine before others, that they may see your good deeds and glorify your Father in heaven."

MATTHEW 5:14–16

Carry each other's burdens, and in this way you will fulfill the law of Christ. . . . Nevertheless, the one who receives instruction in the word should share all good things with their instructor.

GALATIANS 6:2, 6

This is how we know what love is: Jesus Christ laid down his life for us. And we ought to lay down our lives for our brothers and sisters. If anyone has material possessions and sees a brother or sister in need but has no pity on them, how can the love of God be in that person? Dear children, let us not love with words or speech but with actions and in truth.

1 JOHN 3:16–18

Receive from him anything we ask, because we keep his commands and do what pleases him. And this is his command: to believe in the name of his Son, Jesus Christ, and to love one another as he commanded us.

1 JOHN 3:22–23

Fix these words of mine in your hearts and minds; tie them as symbols on your hands and bind them on your foreheads. Teach them to your children, talking about them when you sit at home and when you walk along the road, when you lie down and when you get up.

DEUTERONOMY 11:18–19

My son, keep your father's command
    and do not forsake your mother's teaching. . . .
When you walk, they will guide you;
    when you sleep, they will watch over you;
    when you awake, they will speak to you.
For this command is a lamp,
    this teaching is a light,
and correction and instruction
    are the way to life.

PROVERBS 6:20, 22–23

Love the LORD your God and keep his requirements, his decrees, his laws and his commands always.

DEUTERONOMY 11:1

He said to them, "Go into all the world and preach the gospel to all creation."

"Keep this Book of the Law always on your lips; meditate on it day and night, so that you may be careful to do everything written in it. Then you will be prosperous and successful. Have I not commanded you? Be strong and courageous. Do not be afraid; do not be discouraged, for the LORD your God will be with you wherever you go."

JOSHUA 1:8–9

TRUTH FROM THE BIBLE ABOUT . . .
GOD'S WILL FOR YOUR LIFE

If any of you lacks wisdom, you should ask God, who gives generously to all without finding fault, and it will be given to you.

JAMES 1:5

All the ways of the LORD are loving and faithful
    toward those who keep the demands of his
    covenant.

PSALM 25:10

Your word is a lamp for my feet,
    a light on my path.
I have taken an oath and confirmed it,
    that I will follow your righteous laws.

PSALM 119:105–106

Whether you turn to the right or to the left, your ears will hear a voice behind you, saying, "This is the way; walk in it."

ISAIAH 30:21

Be very careful, then, how you live—not as unwise but as wise, making the most of every opportunity, because the days are evil. Therefore do not be foolish, but understand what the Lord's will is.

EPHESIANS 5:15–17

Rejoice always, pray continually, give thanks in all
circumstances; for this is God's will for you in Christ Jesus.

1 Thessalonians 5:16–18

Teach me to do your will,
    for you are my God;
may your good Spirit
    lead me on level ground.

Psalm 143:10

My son, do not forget my teaching,
    but keep my commands in your heart. . . .
Trust in the LORD with all your heart
    and lean not on your own understanding;
in all your ways submit to him,
    and he will make your paths straight. . . .
My son, do not despise the LORD's discipline,
    and do not resent his rebuke,
because the LORD disciplines those he loves,
    as a father the son he delights in.

Proverbs 3:1, 5–6, 11–12

ANSWERED PRAYER

"Ask and it will be given to you; seek and you will find; knock and the door will be opened to you. For everyone who asks receives; the one who seeks finds; and to the one who knocks, the door will be opened."

MATTHEW 7:7–8

"Again, truly I tell you that if two of you on earth agree about anything they ask for, it will be done for them by my Father in heaven. For where two or three gather in my name, there am I with them."

MATTHEW 18:19–20

Receive from him anything we ask, because we keep his commands and do what pleases him. And this is his command: to believe in the name of his Son, Jesus Christ, and to love one another as he commanded us. The one who keeps God's commands lives in him, and he in them. And this is how we know that he lives in us: We know it by the Spirit he gave us.

1 JOHN 3:22–24

Let us then approach God's throne of grace with confidence, so that we may receive mercy and find grace to help us in our time of need.

HEBREWS 4:16

"Therefore I tell you, whatever you ask for in prayer, believe that you have received it, and it will be yours. And when you stand praying, if you hold anything against anyone, forgive them, so that your Father in heaven may forgive you your sins."

MARK 11:24–25

"And I will do whatever you ask in my name, so that the Father may be glorified in the Son. You may ask me for anything in my name, and I will do it."

JOHN 14:13–14

"But when you pray, go into your room, close the door and pray to your Father, who is unseen. Then your Father, who sees what is done in secret, will reward you."

MATTHEW 6:6

"He will call on me, and I will answer him;
    I will be with him in trouble,
    I will deliver him and honor him.
With long life I will satisfy him
    and show him my salvation."

PSALM 91:15–16

"This is what the LORD says, he who made the earth, the LORD who formed it and established it—the LORD is his name: 'Call to me and I will answer you and tell you great and unsearchable things you do not know.'"

JEREMIAH 33:2–3

SPEAKING GOD'S WORD

"Truly I tell you, if anyone says to this mountain, 'Go, throw yourself into the sea,' and does not doubt in their heart but believes that what they say will happen, it will be done for them."

MARK 11:23

He replied, "If you have faith as small as a mustard seed, you can say to this mulberry tree, 'Be uprooted and planted in the sea,' and it will obey you."

LUKE 17:6

But what does it say? "The word is near you; it is in your mouth and in your heart," that is, the message concerning faith that we proclaim: If you declare with your mouth, "Jesus is Lord," and believe in your heart that God raised him from the dead, you will be saved. For it is with your heart that you believe and are justified, and it is with your mouth that you profess your faith and are saved.

ROMANS 10:8–10

It is written: "I believed; therefore I have spoken." Since we have that same spirit of faith, we also believe and therefore speak, because we know that the one who raised the Lord Jesus from the dead will also raise us with Jesus and present us with you to himself.

2 CORINTHIANS 4:13–14

Instead, speaking the truth in love, we will grow to become in every respect the mature body of him who is the head, that is, Christ.

EPHESIANS 4:15

The wise in heart are called discerning,
 and gracious words promote instruction. . . .
The hearts of the wise make their mouths prudent,
 and their lips promote instruction.
Gracious words are a honeycomb,
 sweet to the soul and healing to the bones.

PROVERBS 16:21, 23–24

The words of the mouth are deep waters,
 but the fountain of wisdom is a rushing stream. . . .
The tongue has the power of life and death,
 and those who love it will eat its fruit.

PROVERBS 18:4, 21

"Whoever acknowledges me before others, I will also acknowledge before my Father in heaven."

MATTHEW 10:32

Let us hold unswervingly to the hope we profess, for he who promised is faithful.

HEBREWS 10:23

FORGIVING OTHERS

"For if you forgive other people when they sin against you, your heavenly Father will also forgive you. But if you do not forgive others their sins, your Father will not forgive your sins."

MATTHEW 6:14–15

Then Peter came to Jesus and asked, "Lord, how many times shall I forgive my brother or sister who sins against me? Up to seven times?"

Jesus answered, "I tell you, not seven times, but seventy-seven times."

MATTHEW 18:21–22

"This is my blood of the covenant, which is poured out for many for the forgiveness of sins."

MATTHEW 26:28

"And when you stand praying, if you hold anything against anyone, forgive them, so that your Father in heaven may forgive you your sins."

MARK 11:25

Bear with each other and forgive one another if any of you has a grievance against someone. Forgive as the Lord forgave you.

COLOSSIANS 3:13

Finally, all of you, be like-minded, be sympathetic, love one another, be compassionate and humble. Do not repay evil with evil or insult with insult. On the contrary, repay evil with blessing, because to this you were called so that you may inherit a blessing.

1 PETER 3:8–9

Get rid of all bitterness, rage and anger, brawling and slander, along with every form of malice. Be kind and compassionate to one another, forgiving each other, just as in Christ God forgave you.

EPHESIANS 4:31–32

Therefore, there is now no condemnation for those who are in Christ Jesus, because through Christ Jesus the law of the Spirit who gives life has set you free from the law of sin and death.

ROMANS 8:1–2

Brothers and sisters, I do not consider myself yet to have taken hold of it. But one thing I do: Forgetting what is behind and straining toward what is ahead, I press on toward the goal to win the prize for which God has called me heavenward in Christ Jesus.

PHILIPPIANS 3:13–14

"So watch yourselves.

"If your brother or sister sins against you, rebuke them; and if they repent, forgive them. Even if they sin against you seven times in a day and seven times come back to you saying 'I repent,' you must forgive them."

LUKE 17:3–4

"Forget the former things;
   do not dwell on the past. . . .
I, even I, am he who blots out
   your transgressions, for my own sake,
   and remembers your sins no more."

ISAIAH 43:18, 25

TRUTH FROM THE BIBLE ABOUT...
GOD'S PLAN OF SALVATION

For all have sinned and fall short of the glory of God, and all are justified freely by his grace through the redemption that came by Christ Jesus.

ROMANS 3:23–24

But God demonstrates his own love for us in this: While we were still sinners, Christ died for us.

ROMANS 5:8

For the wages of sin is death, but the gift of God is eternal life in Christ Jesus our Lord.

ROMANS 6:23

But what does it say? "The word is near you; it is in your mouth and in your heart," that is, the message concerning faith that we proclaim: If you declare with your mouth, "Jesus is Lord," and believe in your heart that God raised him from the dead, you will be saved. For it is with your heart that you believe and are justified, and it is with your mouth that you profess your faith and are saved.

ROMANS 10:8–10

Now, brothers and sisters, I want to remind you of the gospel I preached to you, which you received and on which you have taken your stand. By this gospel you are saved, if you hold firmly to the word I preached to you. Otherwise, you have believed in vain.

For what I received I passed on to you as of first importance: that Christ died for our sins according to the Scriptures, that he was buried, that he was raised on the third day according to the Scriptures.

1 CORINTHIANS 15:1–4

"For God so loved the world that he gave his one and only Son, that whoever believes in him shall not perish but have eternal life. For God did not send his Son into the world to condemn the world, but to save the world through him."

JOHN 3:16–17

For it is by grace you have been saved, through faith—and this is not from yourselves, it is the gift of God—not by works, so that no one can boast.

EPHESIANS 2:8–9

"Here I am! I stand at the door and knock. If anyone hears my voice and opens the door, I will come in and eat with that person, and they with me."

REVELATION 3:20

And this is the testimony: God has given us eternal life, and this life is in his Son. Whoever has the Son has life; whoever does not have the Son of God does not have life.

I write these things to you who believe in the name of the Son of God so that you may know that you have eternal life.

1 John 5:11–13

A FINAL WORD TO THE GRADUATE

As you continue your adventures on this earth, please remember to carry the promises of God with you. Amid all of life's uncertainty, His Word alone is always true, always reliable. Believe in Him. Study His Word. Live His will. And be confident that someday you'll graduate from this life into a new, perfect one in heaven.

*Grace, mercy,
and peace from God
the Father and from Jesus Christ,
the Father's Son, will be with
us in truth and love.*

2 JOHN V. 3